LAWS AND LEGISLATION

# AFFIRMATIVE ACTION AND PREFERENTIAL TREATMENT

## LAWS AND DEVELOPMENTS

# LAWS AND LEGISLATION

Additional books in this series can be found on Nova's website under the Series tab.

Additional e-books in this series can be found on Nova's website under the e-books tab.

LAWS AND LEGISLATION

# AFFIRMATIVE ACTION AND PREFERENTIAL TREATMENT

## LAWS AND DEVELOPMENTS

PAMELA L. MEDINA
AND
JIMMY E. PATEL
EDITORS

nova publishers
*New York*

For permission to use material from this book please contact us:
Telephone 631-231-7269; Fax 631-231-8175
Web Site: http://www.novapublishers.com

## NOTICE TO THE READER



**LIBRARY OF CONGRESS CATALOGING-IN-PUBLICATION DATA**

ISBN: 978-1-62257-465-0

*Published by Nova Science Publishers, Inc. † New York*

# CONTENTS

# PREFACE

This book examines a survey of federal laws containing preferences based on race, gender, or ethnicity. Affirmative action remains a subject of public debate as the result of legal and political developments at the federal, state, and local levels. In recent years, federal courts have reviewed minority admissions programs to state universities; scrutinized the constitutional status of racial diversity policies in public elementary and secondary schools; ruled on minority preferences in public and private employment as a remedy for violation of civil and constitutional rights; and considered federal, state, and local efforts to increase minority participation as contractors and sub-contractors on publicly financed construction projects. Also discussed is affirmative action in the workplace; diversity in public education; race discrimination and the Supreme Court; and pay discrimination claims of the Civil Rights Act.

Chapter 1 – This report provides a broad, but by no means exhaustive, survey of federal statutes that specifically refer to race, gender, or ethnicity as factors to be considered in the administration of any federal program. Such measures may include, but are not limited to, goals, timetables, set-asides, quotas, priorities, and preferences, as those terms are generally (however imperfectly) understood. Based on searches of the LEXIS/NEXIS and WESTLAW legal databases using a variety of search strategies, the compilation seeks to be as comprehensive as possible. With certain noted exceptions, the report collectively describes those statutes found during the course of research that appear, in any manner, to prefer or consider race, gender, or ethnicity as affirmative factors in federal employment, in the award of federal contracts, or in granting any federal benefit to individuals, groups, or institutions. Several laws directed to "socially and economically disadvantaged" individuals, groups, and institutions are included because, as more fully explained by the report, that term has been defined administratively and by statute to presumptively apply to specific racial or ethnic minorities or women.

Chapter 2 – Affirmative action remains a subject of public debate as the result of legal and political developments at the federal, state, and local levels. In recent years, federal courts have reviewed minority admissions programs to state universities; scrutinized the constitutional status of racial diversity policies in public elementary and secondary schools; ruled on minority preferences in public and private employment as a remedy for violation of civil and constitutional rights; and considered federal, state, and local efforts to increase minority participation as contractors and subcontractors on publicly financed construction projects. This report provides a brief history of federal affirmative action law.

Chapter 3 – This report discusses current constitutional and statutory requirements related to affirmative action in employment. Seeds of the legal controversy regarding affirmative action may be traced to the early 1960s as the Supreme Court grappled with the seemingly intractable problem of racial segregation in the nation's public schools. Judicial rulings from this period recognized an "affirmative duty," cast upon local school boards by the Equal Protection Clause of the U.S. Constitution, to desegregate formerly "dual school" systems and to eliminate "root and branch" the last "vestiges" of state-enforced segregation. In the employment context, the Court has similarly upheld the constitutionality of affirmative action plans adopted by or imposed upon governmental entities with a history of past discrimination. Meanwhile, Congress and the Executive have followed the Court's lead by approving a panoply of laws and regulations that authorize, either directly or by judicial or administrative interpretation, "race-conscious" strategies to promote minority opportunity in jobs, education, and governmental contracting.

The basic statutory framework for affirmative action in employment derives from Title VII of the Civil Rights Act of 1964, which prohibits employment discrimination on the basis of race, color, national origin, religion, and sex. The Title VII remedial scheme rests largely on judicial power to order monetary damages and injunctive relief, including "such affirmative action as may be appropriate," to make discrimination victims whole. Except as may be imposed by order of a court to remedy "egregious" violations of law, however, or by consent decree to settle pending claims, there is no general statutory obligation on employers to adopt affirmative action plans. However, the Equal Employment Opportunity Commission

(EEOC) has issued guidelines to protect employers and unions from charges of "reverse discrimination" when they voluntarily take actions to eliminate the effects of past discrimination. In addition, federal departments and agencies are required to periodically formulate affirmative action plans for their employees and a "minority recruitment program" to correct minority "underrepresentation" in specific federal job categories.

The historical model for federal laws and regulations establishing minority participation "goals" may be found in Executive Orders which since the early 1960s have imposed affirmative minority hiring and employment requirements on federally financed construction projects and in connection with other large federal contracts. Executive Order 11246, as presently administered by the Office of Federal Contract Compliance Programs, requires that all employers with 50 or more employees and federal contracts in excess of $50,000 file written affirmative action plans with the government. These must include minority and female hiring goals and timetables to which the contractor must commit its "good faith" efforts.

Chapter 4 – Over a quarter century after the Supreme Court ruling in *Regents of the University of California v. Bakke*, the diversity rationale for affirmative action in public education remains a topic of political and legal controversy. Many colleges and universities have implemented affirmative action policies not only to remedy past discrimination, but also to achieve a racially and ethnically diverse student body or faculty. Justice Powell, in his opinion for the *Bakke* Court, stated that the attainment of a diverse student body is "a constitutionally permissible goal for an institution of higher education," noting that "[t]he atmosphere of 'speculation, experiment, and creation' so essential to the quality of higher education is widely believed to be promoted by a diverse student body." In subsequent years, however, federal courts began to question the Powell rationale, unsettling expectations about the constitutionality of diversity-based affirmative action in educational admissions and faculty hiring.

After a series of conflicting lower court rulings were issued regarding the use of race to promote a diverse student body, the Supreme Court agreed to review the race-conscious admissions policies used by the undergraduate and law school admissions programs at the University of Michigan. In *Grutter v. Bollinger*, a 5 to 4 majority of the Justices held that the University Law School had a "compelling" interest in the "educational benefits that flow from a diverse student body," which justified its race-based efforts to assemble a "critical mass" of "underrepresented" minority students. But in the companion decision, *Gratz v. Bollinger*, six Justices decided that the University's policy of awarding "racial bonus points" to minority applicants was not "narrowly tailored" enough to pass constitutional scrutiny. The decisions resolved, for the time being, the doctrinal muddle left in *Bakke*'s wake. And because the Court's constitutional holdings translate to the private sector under the federal civil rights laws, nonpublic schools, colleges, and universities are likewise affected.

Although the *Grutter* and *Gratz* decisions settled the question of whether race-based policies to promote diversity in higher education are ever constitutionally acceptable, the decisions did not address whether diversity is a permissible goal in the elementary and secondary educational setting. To resolve this question, the Supreme Court agreed to review two cases that involve the use of race to maintain racially diverse public schools and to avoid racial segregation. In a consolidated ruling in *Parents Involved in Community Schools v. Seattle School District No. 1*, the Court struck down the Seattle and Louisville school plans at issue, holding that they violated the equal protection guarantee of the Fourteenth Amendment.

Chapter 5 – This report discusses *Ricci v. DeStefano*, a recent Supreme Court case involving allegations of reverse discrimination by a group of white firefighters who challenged city officials in New Haven, Connecticut, over their refusal to certify a promotional test on which black and Hispanic firefighters had performed poorly relative to white firefighters. In a 5-4 vote, the Court held that the city's actions violated Title VII of the Civil Rights Act of 1964, which prohibits discrimination in employment on the basis of race, color, religion, sex, or national origin. The case has drawn considerable attention, not only because of the controversial nature of the reverse discrimination allegations but also because the Court reversed a decision by a three-judge appellate panel that included Judge Sonia Sotomayor, who was, at the time, a nominee for the Supreme Court and who has since become a member of the Court.

Chapter 6 – This report discusses *Ledbetter v. Goodyear Tire & Rubber Co., Inc.*, a case in which the Supreme Court considered the timeliness of a sex discrimination claim filed under Title VII of the Civil Rights Act, which prohibits employment discrimination on the basis of race, color, religion, sex, or national origin. In *Ledbetter*, the female plaintiff alleged that past sex discrimination had resulted in lower pay increases and that these past pay decisions continued to affect the amount of her pay throughout her employment, resulting in a significant pay disparity between her and her male colleagues by the end of her nearly 20-year career. Under Title VII, a plaintiff is required to file suit within 180 days after an alleged unlawful employment practice has occurred. Although the plaintiff in *Ledbetter* argued that each paycheck she received constituted a new violation of the statute and therefore reset the clock with regard to filing a claim, the Court rejected this argument, reasoning that even if employees suffer continuing effects from past discrimination, their claims are time barred unless filed within the specified number of days of the original discriminatory act. On January 29, 2009, President Obama signed the Lilly Ledbetter Fair Pay Act of 2009 (H.R. 11/S. 181). This legislation supersedes the *Ledbetter* decision by amending Title VII to clarify that the time limit for suing employers for pay discrimination begins each time they issue a paycheck.

In: Affirmative Action and Preferential Treatment ISBN: 978-1-62257-465-0
Editors: P. L. Medina and J. E. Patel 

*Chapter 1*

# SURVEY OF FEDERAL LAWS CONTAINING GOALS, SET-ASIDES, PRIORITIES, OR OTHER PREFERENCES BASED ON RACE, GENDER, OR ETHNICITY*

*Jody Feder, Kate M. Manuel and Julia Taylor*

## SUMMARY

This report provides a broad, but by no means exhaustive, survey of federal statutes that specifically refer to race, gender, or ethnicity as factors to be considered in the administration of any federal program. Such measures may include, but are not limited to, goals, timetables, set-asides, quotas, priorities, and preferences, as those terms are generally (however imperfectly) understood. Based on searches of the LEXIS/NEXIS and WESTLAW legal databases using a variety of search strategies, the compilation seeks to be as comprehensive as possible. With certain noted exceptions, the report collectively describes those statutes found during the course of our research that appear, in any manner, to prefer or consider race, gender, or ethnicity as affirmative factors in federal employment, in the award of federal contracts, or in granting any federal benefit to individuals, groups, or institutions. Several laws directed to "socially and economically disadvantaged" individuals,

* This is an edited, reformatted and augmented version of Congressional Research Service, Publication No. R41038, dated April 14, 2011.

groups, and institutions are included because, as more fully explained by the report, that term has been defined administratively and by statute to presumptively apply to specific racial or ethnic minorities or women.

## INTRODUCTION

The purpose of this report is to provide a broad, but by no means exhaustive, survey of federal statutes that specifically refer to race, gender, or ethnicity as factors to be considered in the administration of any federal program. Such measures may include, but are not limited to, goals, timetables, set-asides, quotas, priorities, and preferences, as those terms are generally (however imperfectly) understood. Based on searches of the LEXIS/NEXIS and WESTLAW legal databases using a variety of search strategies, the compilation reflects our effort to be as comprehensive as possible.[1] Because of the various ways in which such programs can be described, however, we cannot guarantee complete coverage. Moreover, given the disparate policy objectives and wording of the various provisions, some editorial judgment was called for, and the final product may be viewed as over- or under-inclusive, depending on the reader's perspective. Nonetheless, included are any statutes found during the course of our research that appear, in any manner, to prefer or consider race, gender, or ethnicity as affirmative factors in federal employment, in the award of federal contracts, or in granting any federal benefit to individuals or institutions. Several laws directed to "socially and economically disadvantaged" individuals, groups, and institutions are included because, as explained below, that term has been defined administratively and by statute to presumptively apply to specific racial or ethnic minorities or women.[2] However, despite the focus on federal laws containing goals, set-asides, priorities, or other preferences based on race, gender, or ethnicity, this report does not attempt to track whether and how "minority" status, "disadvantage," or other relevant terms are defined by statute, regulation, or case law for purposes of these programs. Those interested in specific programs should check the statutes authorizing and regulations implementing those programs, as well as any case law pertaining to the program, to determine eligibility.

It is important to note that certain categories of federal law are purposely not included. For example, federal regulations and executive orders are generally not covered, although certain regulations and executive orders may be discussed when they apply government-wide or are otherwise significant.

Also not included are various federal civil rights statutes, like Title VI of the 1964 Civil Rights Act and related laws, that place nondiscrimination requirements upon recipients of federal financial assistance without mandating racial, ethnic, or gender preferences *per se*. Nor are regulations of the various federal departments or agencies under Title VI included for the similar reason that, although they almost uniformly authorize "affirmative action" by recipients to "overcome the effects of prior discrimination" or otherwise, they do not explicitly define the obligation in terms of "goals" or "set-asides," or other forms of preference for minorities or women.[3] Also beyond the scope of this study are federal antidiscrimination laws that provide for equal opportunity, such as Title VII of the 1964 Civil Rights Act or the Fair Housing Act.[4] Although many of these statutes authorize "affirmative" relief by the courts in discrimination actions and have been the basis for judicial preference orders in certain circumstances, they do not explicitly direct the imposition of timetables, goals, set-asides, quotas, or preferences on their face.

Another category of statutory preferences excluded from consideration here are federal programs focused solely upon Native Americans living on or near a reservation. Such programs have been upheld by the Supreme Court under the Constitution based on the Government's historical trust relationship with the Tribes and the "unique legal status [of] Indians" in matters relating to tribal affairs "on or near" the reservation.[5] According to the accepted legal view, such "special treatment" constitutes neither "racial discrimination" nor "even a 'racial' preference." It is based instead on a "criterion reasonably designed to further the cause of Indian self-government" which "as applied, is granted to Indians not as a discrete racial group, but, rather, as members of quasi-sovereign tribal entities...."[6] Native American individuals and Indian tribes are among those eligible for some of the programs listed, such as the Minority Small Business and Capital Development Program, but programs open only to Native Americans are generally not included.[7]

We also focused on programs that would arguably directly benefit minorities or women and thus excluded requirements that federal agencies report certain information on their programs for minorities or women to Congress or congressional committees.[8] Such provisions arguably indirectly benefit minorities and women by making agencies accountable for any apparent failures to deal with minorities or women, but they seem less certain to provide assistance to minorities and women than the other programs and provisions included here. Likewise, we exclude programs that focus exclusively on pregnant women, since these programs are not explicitly based on gender.

Below, this report sets forth the various preference programs, organized into two main sections: government-wide programs and agency-specific programs, which are subdivided by agency.[9]

## Government-Wide Programs

This section lists programs involving "preferential" treatment of minorities or women that multiple federal agencies have a role in implementing. It does not address statutes without explicit racial, gender, or ethnicity classifications that agencies could potentially implement in such a way as to prefer minorities or women.[10] Because many of these programs are known by their names, they are listed here alphabetically by name, when possible, with their statutory authorities noted parenthetically after their names.

Affirmative Action Plans (Executive Order 11246, as amended by Executive Orders 11375, 11478, 12086, 12107, and 13279, as well as partially superseded by Executive Order 11478): Requires all non-construction federal prime contractors or subcontractors with 50 or more employees that receive more than $50,000 from the government in any twelve month period to develop written affirmative action plans for each of their establishments. Additionally, agencies cannot award or modify non-construction contracts valued at $10 million or more unless the Office of Federal Contract Compliance Programs at the Department of Labor determines in writing that the contractor is compliant with Executive Order 11246. Construction contractors are subject to separate affirmative action requirements, including having "goals for minority and female participation, expressed in percentage terms for the [c]ontractor's aggregate workforce in each trade on all construction work in the covered area" incorporated as terms of the contract.[11]

Agency Forecasts (15 U.S.C. § 637(a)(12)(C)(i)-(iii)): Requires agencies with contract actions worth $50 million or more per fiscal year to prepare "forecast[s] of expected contract opportunities or classes of contract opportunities for the next and succeeding fiscal years that small business concerns, including those owned and controlled by socially and economically disadvantaged individuals, are capable of performing." To the extent that such information is available, such forecasts shall include (1) the approximate number of individual contract opportunities; (2) the approximate dollar value, or range of dollar values, for each contract opportunity or class of contract opportunities; (3) the anticipated time for issuance of a procurement request (by fiscal quarter); and (4) the activity responsible for award and administration of the contract.

Goaling Program (15 U.S.C. § 644(g)(1)-(2)): Requires the President to set government-wide goals for the percentage of federal contract dollars awarded to various types of small businesses, including small disadvantaged businesses (SDBs) and women-owned small businesses (WOSBs).

The goals for each category should be "not less than 5 percent of the total value of all prime contract and subcontract awards."[12] Agency heads must set similar, agency-specific goals for contracting and subcontracting with SBDs and WOSBs in consultation with the Small Business Administration (SBA) Administrator. The agency-specific goals do not need to meet or exceed any specific percentage. Rather, they are to "realistically reflect the potential" of small businesses to perform federal prime contracts and subcontracts and thus vary among agencies.[13]

Grants and Cooperative Agreements with State and Local Governments (OMB Circular A102): Establishes a national policy to award a "fair share of contracts" to small and minority business firms, as well as requires grantees to take "similar appropriate affirmative action to support women's enterprises."

Minority Small Business and Capital Development Program (8(a) Program) (15 U.S.C. § 636(j); 15 U.S.C. § 637(a)): Provides various benefits for participating small businesses, which must be at least 51% owned and controlled by socially and economically disadvantaged individuals or groups. Benefits include (1) set-aside and sole-source contracts with federal agencies; (2) direct and guaranteed loans from the SBA; (3) transfer of technology and surplus property owned by the United States; (4) management and technical assistance, including training in financing, management, accounting, bookkeeping, marketing, the operation of small businesses, and the identification and development of new business opportunities; and (5) participation in an SBA-sponsored mentor-protégé program, with mentors providing protégés with technical or management assistance; financial assistance in the form of equity investments or loans; subcontracts; or assistance in performing prime contracts with the government in the form of joint venture arrangements.[14]

Small Business Innovation Research (SBIR) Program (15 U.S.C. § 638): Requires every federal department with a research and development budget of $100 million or more to operate an SBIR program, which seeks, among other things, to increase the involvement of SDBs in the process of technological innovation.[15]

Small Business Subcontracting Program (15 U.S.C. § 637(d)): Promotes the use of SDBs and WOSBs as subcontractors on federal prime contracts. Agencies must include clauses obligating the contractor to carry out the federal policy of ensuring that SBDs and WOSBs have "the maximum practicable opportunity to participate in [contract] performance" in all eligible contracts valued at over $150,000.[16] Agencies must also negotiate subcontracting plans with the apparently successful offeror before awarding, amending, or modifying any eligible contract valued at over $650,000 ($1.5 million for construction contracts for public facilities). Subcontracting plans must include percentage goals for the use of SDBs and WOSBs, among others, as subcontractors and describe the efforts the offeror will make to ensure that such businesses "have an equitable opportunity to compete for subcontracts."[17] Agencies cannot award an eligible contract unless the subcontracting plan has been agreed upon and is incorporated into the contract. The plan constitutes a "material part of the contract,"[18] and a contractor's failure to comply in good faith with it constitutes a material breach, potentially requiring the contractor to pay liquidated damages.[19] Agencies must consider contractors' performance on the goals listed in their subcontracting plans when evaluating past performance.[20] Past performance is considered (1) as an evaluation factor in negotiated procurements; (2) when determining whether prospective contractors are sufficiently "responsible" to be awarded a federal contract; and (3) when determining award fees. Performance in subcontracting with SDBs, WOSBs, and other small businesses is the only factor that agencies *must* consider when evaluating past performance.

Small Disadvantaged Business Participation Program (48 C.F.R. §§ 19.1201-19.1202-4): Authorizes agencies to use the following "evaluation factors," focused upon subcontracting with SDBs, when awarding prime contracts: (1) the extent to which the offers specifically identify potential subcontracting opportunities for SDBs; (2) the extent of offerors' commitment to use SDBs; (3) the complexity and variety of work to be performed by small SDBs; (4) the realism of offerors' proposals; (5) the offerors' past performance in complying with subcontracting plan goals for SDBs and monetary targets for SDB participation; and (6) the extent of SDB participation in terms of the value of the total acquisition. Agencies also have authority to incorporate "monetary incentives" for subcontracting with SDBs into their prime contracts. Such incentives reward prime contractors by paying them up to 10% of the amount by which their performance in subcontracting with SBDs exceeds their targets for subcontracting with SDBs.

Uniform Administrative Requirements for Grants and Agreements with Institutions of Higher Education, Hospitals and Other Nonprofit Organizations (OMB Circular A-110): Requires agencies to encourage funding recipients to use women-owned and minority-owned banks as a way of promoting the "national goal of expanding the opportunities for women-owned and minority-owned business enterprises."

Women-Owned Small Business Program (15 U.S.C. § 637(m)): Authorizes agencies to "restrict competition for any contract for the procurement of goods and services by the Federal government to small business concerns owned and controlled by women" when certain conditions are met.[21] These conditions require that (1) the small business be at least 51% owned by one or more women who are economically disadvantaged; (2) the contracting officer reasonably expects that offers will be obtained from at least two responsible small businesses offering the products of different small businesses and the award will be made at a fair market price; (3) the anticipated value of the contract will not exceed $3 million ($5 million for manufacturing contracts); and (4) the proposed contract is for the procurement of goods or services in an industry in which the SBA has determined that WOSBs are underrepresented.[22]

41 U.S.C. § 1122: Requires the Office of Federal Procurement Policy (OFPP)[23] to develop policies, in consultation with the SBA Administrator, that ensure that SDBs and WOSBs "are provided with the maximum practicable opportunities to participate in procurements that are conducted for amounts below the simplified acquisition threshold" (generally $150,000) [24] and promote achievement of the government-wide and agency-specific goals for contracting and subcontracting with SDBs and WOSBs.

41 U.S.C. § 2301: Requires that agency electronic commerce systems, technologies, procedures, and processes facilitate access to federal procurement opportunities for SDBs and WOSBs, among others.

## AGENCY-SPECIFIC PROGRAMS

### Agriculture

**7 U.S.C. § 450i**: Establishes competitive, special, and facilities research grants. The Secretary of Agriculture may assist in the development of capabilities in the agricultural, food, and environmental sciences by "ensur[ing] that the faculty of small, mid-sized, and minority-serving institutions who have not previously been successful in obtaining competitive grants under this subsection receive a portion of the grants."

**7 U.S.C. § 1524**: Requires the Secretary to place "special emphasis" on risk management strategies, education, and outreach to specifically targeted groups, including socially disadvantaged farmers and ranchers, in carrying out programs on crop insurance and risk management education.

**7 U.S.C. § 1531**: Provides for a waiver of minimum risk management purchase requirements for certain socially disadvantaged livestock producers, farmers, and ranchers.

**7 U.S.C. § 1632a**: Establishes value-added agricultural product market development grants. The Secretary must give priority in awarding these grants to projects that contribute to increasing opportunities for certain groups, including socially disadvantaged farmers and ranchers. The Secretary also must reserve 10% of the amounts made available for each fiscal year to fund projects that benefit beginning farmers or ranchers or socially disadvantaged farmers or ranchers.

**7 U.S.C. § 1924**: Establishes the conservation loan and loan guarantee program. The Secretary is required to "give priority" to qualified beginning farmers or ranchers and socially disadvantaged farmers or ranchers, among other groups, when making or guaranteeing loans under this section.

**7 U.S.C. § 1932(c)**: Establishes rural cooperative development grants, for which appropriations of $50 million for each of fiscal years 2008 through 2012 have been authorized. If the total amount appropriated for a fiscal year exceeds $7.5 million, the Secretary must reserve an amount equal to 20% of the total amount appropriated for grants for cooperative development centers, individual cooperatives, or groups of cooperatives that serve socially disadvantaged groups and a majority of whose boards of directors or governing boards are comprised of individuals who are members of socially disadvantaged groups.

**7 U.S.C. § 1935**: Establishes a program to provide loans to qualified beginning farmers or ranchers and socially disadvantaged farmers or ranchers for down payments on farm ownership loans. The Secretary, "to the maximum extent practicable," shall (1) encourage retiring farmers and ranchers to assist in the sale of their farms and ranches to qualified beginning farmers or ranchers and socially disadvantaged farmers or ranchers by providing seller financing; (2) coordinate the loan program established by this section with state programs that provide farm ownership or operating loans for beginning farmers or ranchers or socially disadvantaged farmers or ranchers; and (3) establish annual performance goals to promote the use of the down payment loan program and other joint financing arrangements as the preferred choice for direct real estate loans made by any lender to a qualified beginning farmer or rancher or socially disadvantaged farmer or rancher.

**7 U.S.C. § 1936**: Establishes the beginning farmer or rancher and socially disadvantaged farmer or rancher contract land sales program. Subject to eligibility requirements and some limitations, the Secretary is to guarantee loans made by private sellers of farms or ranches to qualified beginning farmers or ranchers or socially disadvantaged farmers or ranchers.

**7 U.S.C. § 1985**: Establishes the order and method of sale for the Secretary in offering to sell real property that is acquired through security servicing. Not later than 135 days after acquiring real property, the Secretary shall offer to sell the property to a qualified beginning farmer or rancher or a socially disadvantaged farmer or rancher at current market value based on a current appraisal. "To the maximum extent practicable, the Secretary shall maximize the opportunity for beginning farmers or ranchers and socially disadvantaged farmers or ranchers to purchase real property acquired by the Secretary under this title by combining or dividing inventory parcels of the property in such manner as the Secretary determines to be appropriate." This section also permits the leasing of property to beginning farmers or ranchers or socially disadvantaged farmers or ranchers for farms or ranches acquired by the Secretary if the beginning farmer or rancher or the socially disadvantaged farmer or rancher qualifies for a credit sale or direct farm ownership loan.

**7 U.S.C. § 2000**: Establishes a "homestead protection" program, under which, at any time during the period of occupancy of a borrower-owner who is a socially disadvantaged farmer or rancher, the borrower-owner, or a member of his or her immediate family, shall "have a right of first refusal to reacquire the homestead property on such terms and conditions as the Secretary shall determine, except that the Secretary may not demand a payment for the homestead property that is in excess of the current market value of the homestead property as established by an independent appraisal."

**7 U.S.C. § 2003**: Requires the Secretary to establish annual target participation rates that ensure members of socially disadvantaged groups receive loans and have the opportunity to purchase or lease inventory farmland.

**7 U.S.C. § 2016(h)**: Prohibits the Secretary from approving an electronic benefits transfer system for the food stamp program in which households must participate unless "a sufficient number of eligible retail food stores, including those stores able to serve minority language populations, have agreed to participate in the system throughout the area in which it will operate to ensure that eligible households will not suffer a significant reduction in their choice of retail food stores or a significant increase in the cost of food or transportation to participating food stores."

**7 U.S.C. § 2204b**: Directs the Secretary to prepare a comprehensive rural development strategy based on the needs, goals, objectives, plans, and recommendations of local communities, sub-state areas, states, and multistate regions. Such strategy must "take into account the need to improve the economic well-being of all rural residents and alleviate the problems of low income, elderly, minority, and otherwise disadvantaged rural residents."

**7 U.S.C. § 2279**: Requires the Secretary of Agriculture to "carry out an outreach and technical assistance program to encourage and assist socially disadvantaged farmers and ranchers ... in owning and operating farms and ranches ... [and] in participating equitably in the full range of agricultural programs offered by the Department."

**7 U.S.C. § 2279a**: Requires the Secretary to adjust the bases and yields and make available any appropriate commodity program benefits if he or she determines that crop acreage bases or farm program payment yields established for farms owned or operated by socially disadvantaged producers were not established in accordance with the law. The Secretary shall also make such changes in the administration of the Consolidated Farm and Rural Development Act as are deemed necessary "to provide for the fair and equitable treatment of socially disadvantaged producers" if it is determined that application of the act with respect to such producers is inconsistent with the act's requirements.

**7 U.S.C. § 3151**: Establishes grants to enhance research capacity in schools of veterinary medicine. The Secretary may set aside a portion of funds appropriated for the award of grants under this section for grants to eligible colleges and universities that the Secretary determines have "unique capabilities for achieving the objective of full participation of minority groups in research in the Nation's schools of veterinary medicine."

**7 U.S.C. § 3152**: Establishes grants and fellowships for food and agricultural sciences education. The Secretary may set aside a portion of the funds appropriated for the awarding of grants to eligible colleges and universities (including the University of the District of Columbia) that the Secretary "determines have unique capabilities for achieving the objective of full representation of minority groups in the food and agricultural sciences workforce, or in the rural economic, community, and business development workforce, of the United States."

**7 U.S.C. § 3241**: Authorizes the Secretary to make grants to Hispanic-serving institutions (HSIs) for the purpose of promoting and strengthening the ability of such institutions to carry out education, applied research, and related community development programs.

**7 U.S.C. § 3319f**: Establishes grants for the beginning farmer and rancher development program. Not less than 25% of the funds used to carry out this provision for a fiscal year shall be used to support programs and services that address the needs of socially disadvantaged beginning farmers or ranchers.

**7 U.S.C. § 5331**: Requires that the National Nutrition Monitoring Advisory Council include representatives of minority organizations, among others.

**7 U.S.C. § 5923(c)**: Establishes grants for the rural electronic commerce extension program and specifies that selection criteria for such grants shall include "the extent of participation of low-income and minority businesses or microenterprises in a proposed project or activity under the extension program." A development center or grant applicant must obtain contributions from nonfederal sources of an amount equal to 50% of the grant amount, although this amount may be reduced to 25% if the grant recipient serves low-income or minority-owned businesses or microenterprises.

**7 U.S.C. § 5925**: Establishes high-priority research and extension areas. Research and extension grants may be made under this section to increase participation by women and underrepresented minorities from rural areas in the fields of science, technology, engineering, and mathematics, with priority given to eligible institutions that carry out continuing programs funded by the Secretary.

**7 U.S.C. § 6934**: Establishes the Office of Advocacy and Outreach within the Department of Agriculture, whose duties include ensuring small farms and ranches, beginning farmers and ranchers, and socially disadvantaged farmers and ranchers have access to and participate equitably in Department programs and services. The Secretary is also required to establish the Socially Disadvantaged Farmers Group within the Office.

**7 U.S.C. § 7625**: Authorizes the Secretary to give priority to socially disadvantaged farmers when awarding grants in support of the national food safety training, education, extension, outreach, and technical assistance program.

**7 U.S.C. § 8111**: Establishes the Biomass Crop Assistance Program (BCAP) and requires the Secretary to provide financial assistance to producers of eligible crops in BCAP project areas. In selecting BCAP project areas, the Secretary shall consider socially disadvantaged farmers or ranchers.

**7 U.S.C. § 8711**: Excludes socially disadvantaged farmers and ranchers from provisions on the treatment of farms with limited base acres.

**7 U.S.C. § 8752**: Excludes socially disadvantaged farmers or ranchers from provisions on the treatment of farms with limited base acres for peanut farms.

**16 U.S.C. §§ 3835(f), 3841(a)(1)(B)**: Provide additional transition options for socially disadvantaged farmers and ranchers under the agricultural resources conservation program in order to facilitate the transfer of land subject to contracts from retired or retiring owners and operators to beginning farmers or ranchers and socially disadvantaged farmers or ranchers.

**16 U.S.C. §§ 3839aa-2, 3841(g)(1)(B)**: Limit increases in payments for socially disadvantaged farmers and ranchers under the agricultural resources conservation program.

**16 U.S.C. § 3844**: Allows the Secretary to offer "incentives" for socially disadvantaged farmers and ranchers to participate in conservation programs.

**19 U.S.C. § 2497**: Provides for waivers for socially disadvantaged farmers and ranchers under a supplemental agricultural disaster assistance program.

**42 U.S.C. § 3020e-1**: Authorizes the Assistant Secretary to award grants to entities that establish pension counseling and information outreach programs for "women, minorities, older individuals residing in rural areas and low income retirees, and older individuals with limited English proficiency."

## Banking

**12 U.S.C. § 635:** Establishes the powers and functions of the Export-Import Bank. Among its duties, the Bank shall be responsible for advising small businesses of opportunities, with particular emphasis on conducting outreach and increasing loans to socially and economically disadvantaged small businesses, WOSBs, and small businesses employing fewer than 100 employees and on liaising with the SBA and other departments and agencies on matters affecting small businesses.

**12 U.S.C. § 635a:** Establishes an office whose sole function is to continue and enhance the outreach activities of the Bank with respect to, and increase the total amount of loans, guarantees, and insurance provided by the Bank to support, exports by socially and economically disadvantaged small businesses and WOSBs within the Small Business Division. The President of the Bank must ensure, to the maximum extent practicable, that qualified minority and women applicants are considered when filling positions.

**12 U.S.C. § 635a-4:** Requires the Board of Directors of the Export-Import Bank to attempt to ensure that a major share of any loan guarantee ultimately serves to promote exports from small, medium-size, and minority businesses or agricultural concerns.

**12 U.S.C. § 1441**: Requires the Financing Corporation to ensure that minority-owned or - controlled commercial banks, investment banking firms, underwriters, and bond counsels have an opportunity to "participate to a significant degree" in any public offering of obligations it issues.

**12 U.S.C. § 1441a:** Authorizes the Resolution Trust Corporation (RTC) to award minority- and women-owned businesses "an additional 10 percent of the total technical points and an additional 5 percent of the total cost preference points achievable in the technical and cost rating process" when evaluating proposals for contracts. RTC must establish guidelines for "achieving the goal of a reasonably even distribution of contracts awarded to the various subgroups of the class of minority- and women-owned businesses and minority- and women-owned law firms whose total number of certified contractors comprise not less than 5 percent of all minority- and women-owned certified contractors." This provision also includes requirements to (1) promote the acquisition of branch facilities in minority neighborhoods by minority depository institutions; (2) provide assistance to minority-owned depository institutions and minority investors in acquiring savings associations for which the RTC has been appointed conservator or receiver; (3) establish a minority interim capital assistance program; and (4) give offers from minority individuals, minority-owned businesses, or minority depository institutions "preference" when considering offers to acquire any insured depository institution, or branch thereof, located in a minority neighborhood.

**12 U.S.C. § 1441b:** Requires the Thrift Depositor Protection Oversight Board to ensure that minority-owned or -controlled commercial banks, investment banking firms, underwriters, and bond counsels have an opportunity to participate to a significant degree in any public or negotiated offering of obligations it issues.

**12 U.S.C. § 1823(f)(12):** Authorizes Federal Deposit Insurance Corporation (FDIC) approval of minority-controlled bank acquisitions by minority-controlled holding companies without regard to asset size.

**12 U.S.C. § 1831q:** Requires the FDIC to periodically provide to a wide range of minority- and women-owned businesses and nonprofit organizations more than 50% controlled by minority individuals that provide affordable housing with information that is "sufficient to inform such businesses and organizations of availability and terms of financing."

**12 U.S.C. § 1833e:** Requires that the FDIC, the Comptroller of the Currency, and the Federal Housing Finance Board each prescribe regulations "to establish and oversee a minority outreach program ... to ensure inclusion ... of minorities and women" in all agency contracts.

**12 U.S.C. § 2219c:** Requires that all institutions within the Farm Credit System with more than 20 employees establish and maintain affirmative action plans that "appl[y] the affirmative action standards otherwise applied to contractors of the Federal Government."

**12 U.S.C. § 2279aa-6:** Requires the Federal Agricultural Mortgage Corporation to ensure that, as a condition of providing any guarantees, facilities take "such steps as may be necessary to ensure that minority owned or controlled investment banking firms, underwriters, and bond counsels ... have an opportunity to participate to a significant degree in any public offering of securities."

**12 U.S.C. § 2903:** Allows federal financial supervisory agencies examining the record of nonminority-owned and non-women-owned financial institutions in "meeting the credit needs of its entire community, including low- and moderate-income neighborhoods" to consider capital investment, loan participation, and other ventures undertaken by the institution in cooperation with minority- and women-owned financial institutions and low-income credit unions provided that these activities help meet the credit needs of local communities in which such institutions and credit unions are chartered.

**12 U.S.C. § 2907**: Provides that any donation or sale on favorable terms of a bank branch in a minority neighborhood to a minority- or women-owned depository institution shall be a factor in determining the compliance of the selling or donating institution with the Community Reinvestment Act.

**12 U.S.C. § 4520:** Requires the Federal National Mortgage Association, the Federal Home Loan Mortgage Corporation, and any Federal Home Loan Bank to establish minority outreach programs to "ensure the inclusion (to the maximum extent possible) in contracts entered into by the enterprises of minorities ... and women and businesses owned by minorities and women ..., including financial institutions, investment banking firms, underwriters, accountants, brokers, and providers of legal services."

**12 U.S.C. § 4703:** Establishes the National Fund for Community Development Banking and creates a 15-member advisory board, which includes nine private citizens appointed by the President who shall be selected, to the maximum extent practicable, to provide for national geographic representation and racial, ethnic, and gender diversity.

**12 U.S.C. § 5217:** Requires the Secretary of the Treasury to develop and implement standards and procedures to ensure, to the maximum extent practicable, the inclusion and utilization of minorities, women, and minority- and women-owned businesses in any solicitation or contract under the Troubled Assets Relief Program for which the Secretary has waived any provisions of the Federal Acquisition Regulation pertaining to minority contracting.

**12 U.S.C. § 5452:** Requires the "Departmental Offices of the Department of the Treasury," Federal Deposit Insurance Corporation, Federal Housing Finance Agency, Federal Reserve banks, Board of Governors of the Federal Reserve System, National Credit Union Administration, Office of the Comptroller of the Currency, Securities and Exchange Commission, and Bureau of Consumer Financial Protection each to establish an Office of Minority and Women Inclusion, with responsibility for all matters of the agency relating to diversity. The directors of these Offices are to develop and implement standards and procedures to ensure, to the maximum extent possible, the fair inclusion and utilization of minorities, women, and minority- and women-owned businesses in activities of the agency, including the performance of any contracts. Contract proposals shall be evaluated, "to the extent consistent with applicable law," in part, based upon the diversity of the applicant, and contractors shall ensure, to the maximum extent practicable, the fair inclusion of minorities and women in their workforce and as subcontractors. Contractors or subcontractors who fail to make good faith efforts to include minorities and women may be terminated.

## Commerce

**15 U.S.C. § 278g-5**: Authorizes the Director of the National Institute of Standards and Technology to work with industry, trade associations, professional societies, and others to "raise awareness in the United States, including awareness by businesses that are majority owned by women, minorities, or both, of enterprise integration activities in the United States and abroad, including by the convening of conferences."

**15 U.S.C. § 3704**: Requires the Secretary of Commerce to establish a Minority Serving Institution Digital and Wireless Technology Opportunity Program to enable eligible minority-serving institutions of higher education to acquire and augment their use of digital and wireless networking technologies to improve the quality and delivery of educational services.

**15 U.S.C. §§ 7101 et seq.**: Establish the Interagency Committee on Women's Business Enterprise, which is to "[p]romote, coordinate and monitor the plans, programs and operations of the departments and agencies of the Executive Branch which may contribute to the establishment, preservation and strengthening of women's business enterprise." The SBA Administrator must ensure, "to the extent possible," that the Committee's appointed members reflect geographic, racial, economic, and sectoral diversity.

**15 U.S.C. § 7404**: Requires the Director of the National Science Foundation (NSF) to establish a program to award grants to minority-serving and other institutions of higher education "to establish or improve undergraduate and master's degree programs in computer and network security [and] to increase the number of students, including the number of students from groups historically underrepresented in these fields."

**15 U.S.C. § 7501**: Establishes the National Nanotechnology Program and creates interdisciplinary nanotechnology research centers, which are to (1) be established, "to the greatest extent possible," in geographically diverse locations; (2) encourage the participation of Historically Black Colleges and Universities (HBCUs) and minority institutions, and (3) include institutions located in states participating in the Experimental Program to Stimulate Competitive Research.

**19 U.S.C. § 2511(f)**: Specifies that the President's authority to waive "discriminatory purchasing requirements" in government procurement does not authorize waiver of "preferences" for minorities or small businesses.

**42 U.S.C. § 6705**: Prohibits grants for local public works projects from being made unless "the applicant gives satisfactory assurance to the Secretary that at least 10 per centum of the amount of each grant shall be expended for minority business enterprises" or the Secretary determines otherwise.

## Communications

**47 U.S.C. §§ 309(i)(3)(A), 309(j)(4)(D)**: Require the Federal Communications Commission (FCC) to "establish rules and procedures to ensure that, in the administration of any system of random selection ... used for granting licenses or construction permits for any media of mass communications, significant preferences will be granted to applicants or groups of applicants, the grant to which of the license or permit would increase the diversification of ownership of the media of mass communications. To further diversify the ownership of media of mass communications, an additional significant preference shall be granted to any applicant controlled by a member or members of a minority group." The FCC must also prescribe regulations for use in radio licensing proceedings that "ensure that small businesses, rural telephone companies, and businesses owned by members of minority groups and women are given the opportunity to participate in the provision of spectrum-based services, and, for such purposes, consider the use of tax certificates, bidding preferences, and other procedures."

**47 U.S.C. §§ 392, § 393**: Establish grants for the construction of public telecommunications facilities. The Secretary of Commerce must "give special consideration" to applications that would increase ownership of, operation of, and participation in public telecommunications entities by minorities and women. The Secretary is also required to "take affirmative steps" to inform minorities and women of the availability of funds and the localities where new public telecommunications facilities are needed, and to "provide such other assistance and information as may be appropriate."

**47 U.S.C. § 396(a)(6)**: Directs the Corporation for Public Broadcasting to "encourage the development of programming ... that addresses the needs of unserved and underserved audiences, particularly children and minorities."

**47 U.S.C. § 532(i)**: Provides for programming from qualified minority or educational programming sources.

**47 U.S.C. § 554**: Establishes equal employment opportunity requirements for any corporation, partnership, association, joint-stock company, or trust engaged primarily in the management or operation of cable systems.

**47 U.S.C. § 1305(h)(3):** Gives SDBs special consideration in the selection of grant recipients under the Broadband Technology Opportunities Program funded by the American Recovery and Reinvestment Act.

## Defense

**10 U.S.C. § 1722(h)**: Requires the Secretary of Defense or the Secretary of a military department to, consistent with the merit system principles, take into consideration the need to maintain a balanced workforce in which women and members of racial and ethnic minority groups are appropriately represented in Government service when developing acquisition workforce policies.

**10 U.S.C. § 2191**: Requires the Secretary of Defense to take "appropriate action" to encourage applications for National Defense Science and Engineering Graduate Fellowships from persons who are members of groups, including minority groups, women, and disabled persons that have historically been underrepresented in the science and technology fields.

**10 U.S.C. § 2193**: Requires the Secretary of Defense to give priority to awarding grants for higher education in science and mathematics "in a manner likely to stimulate the interest of women and members of minority groups in pursuing scientific and engineering careers."

**10 U.S.C. § 2194**: Requires that Department of Defense (DOD) laboratories give "priority" to entering into education partnership agreements with HBCUs and other minority institutions.

**10 U.S.C. § 2196(j)(8)**: Specifies that the selection criteria for the manufacturing engineering grant program established by the Secretary of Defense must require proposals "to achieve a significant level of participation by women, members of minority groups, and individuals with disabilities through active recruitment of students from among such persons."

**10 U.S.C. §§ 2302 note, 2303 note**: Establish a temporary DOD Mentor-Protégé Program to encourage major DOD contractors to furnish SDBs with assistance designed to enhance their capabilities to perform as subcontractors and suppliers under DOD contracts. Mentors may provide a range of assistance to protégés, including general business management assistance, progress payments under subcontracts, advance payments, loans, and cash in exchange for ownership interests in protégé firms.

**10 U.S.C. § 2304(b)(2)**: Authorizes defense agencies, the National Aeronautics and Space Administration (NASA), and the Coast Guard, to set aside procurements for competitions in which only small businesses, HBCUs, and minority institutions can participate in order to further the purposes of 10 U.S.C. § 2323.

**10 U.S.C. § 2323**: Establishes as a goal that 5% of the contract dollars of DOD, NASA, and the Coast Guard be awarded to SDBs each year. Section 2323 also authorizes these agencies to "enter into contracts using less than full and open competitive procedures (including awards under section 8(a) of the Small Business Act) and partial set asides," as well as make price evaluation adjustments of up to 10% to offers of SDBs.[25] The U.S. Court of Appeals for the Federal Circuit found this provision facially unconstitutional in its November 2008 decision in *Rothe Development Corporation v. Department of Defense*,[26] and agencies have since been barred from implementing any programs under its authority.[27] However, legislation enacted by the first session of the 111$^{th}$ Congress restored defense agencies' authority to provide certain forms of technical and infrastructure assistance to minority-serving institutions of higher education, including HBCUs, HSIs, Alaska Native- and

Native Hawaiian-serving institutions (ANNHIs), and other minority institutions.[28]

**10 U.S.C. § 2362**: Requires the Secretary of Defense, acting through the Director of Defense Research and Engineering and the Secretary of each military department, to carry out a program to provide assistance to covered educational institutions, including accredited postsecondary minority institutions, to assist the Department in defense-related research, development, testing, and evaluation activities. The Secretary is also authorized to implement a program assisting HBCUs and other minority-serving institutions of higher education to participate in defense-related research, testing, and evaluation activities through the competitive awarding of grants, cooperative agreements, contracts, scholarships, fellowships, or the acquisition of research equipment or instrumentation, among other means.

**10 U.S.C. § 2687 note**: Requires the Secretary of Defense to give preference "to the greatest extent practicable" to SDBs when entering contracts with private entities as part of the closure or realignment of a military installation under a base closure law.

**10 U.S.C. § 2904(b)(2)**: Specifies that the Strategic Environmental Research and Development Program Scientific Advisory Board shall consist of "persons who are eminent in the fields of basic sciences, engineering, ocean and environmental sciences, education, research management, international and security affairs, health physics, health sciences, or social sciences with due regard given to the equitable representation of scientists and engineers who are women or who represent a minority group."

**10 U.S.C. § 4552(5)**: Articulates a federal policy of providing, "as appropriate," small businesses, including socially and economically disadvantaged small businesses and new small businesses, with "incentives that encourage those businesses to undertake manufacturing and other industrial processing activities that contribute to the prosperity of the United States."

**10 U.S.C. § 4553**: Creates the Armament Retooling and Manufacturing Support (ARMS) Initiative, whose purposes include increasing opportunities for small businesses, including socially and economically disadvantaged small businesses and new small businesses, to use eligible facilities for ARMS-related purposes.

**33 U.S.C. § 544c**: Directs the Secretary of the Army, acting through the Chief of Engineers, to "make a maximum effort to assure the full participation of members of minority groups, living in the States participating in the Tennessee-Tombigbee Waterway Development Authority," in the construction of the Tennessee-Tombigbee Waterway project, including encouraging the use of minority-owned firms whenever possible.

**44 U.S.C. § 502 note**: Requires the Public Printer to establish a "test program," ending on October 1, 2000, to increase the number of contracts for printing, binding, and related services for DOD awarded to SDBs, HBCUs, and minority institutions. The goal for the program was that the amount of such contracts should be "equivalent to not more than 5 percent of the value of the printing, binding, and related services which were procured in the preceding fiscal year by the Government Printing Office from non-Government sources" for DOD.

**50 U.S.C. § 403 note**: Requires the Director of Central Intelligence to carry out and report to Congress on a three-year pilot project to test and evaluate alternative, innovative methods to promote equality of employment opportunities within the intelligence community for women, minorities, and individuals with diverse ethnic and cultural backgrounds, skills, language proficiency, and expertise.

**50 U.S.C. § 403-1**: Requires the Director of National Intelligence, in consultation with the heads of other agencies or elements of the intelligence community, to prescribe personnel policies and programs applicable to the intelligence community that "ensure that the personnel of the intelligence community are sufficiently diverse for purposes of the collection and analysis of intelligence through the recruitment and training of women, minorities, and individuals with diverse ethnic, cultural, and linguistic backgrounds."

**50 U.S.C. § 1902**: Requires that the Secretary of Defense or any contract organization selecting the recipients of scholarships, fellowships, or grants awarded pursuant to this title "take into consideration" (1) the extent to which the selections will result in there being an equitable geographic distribution of scholarships, fellowships, or grants and (2) the extent to which the distribution of scholarships and fellowships to individuals reflects the cultural, racial, and ethnic diversity of the U.S. population.

## Education

**20 U.S.C. § 954**: Provides that, in selecting individuals and groups of exceptional talent as recipients of financial assistance provided under this subsection, the Chairperson of the National Endowment for the Arts (NEA) shall give particular regard to artists and artistic groups that have traditionally been underrepresented.

**20 U.S.C. § 955**: Requires the President to give "due regard" to the equitable representation of women, minorities, and individuals with disabilities who are involved in the arts when making appointments to the National Council on the Arts and make appointments so as to represent equitably all geographical areas in the United States.

**20 U.S.C. § 956**: Requires the Chairperson of the National Endowment for the Humanities to give "particular regard" to scholars and educational and cultural institutions that have traditionally been underrepresented when selecting individuals and groups of exceptional talent as recipients of financial assistance provided under this subsection.

**20 U.S.C. § 957**: Requires the President to give "due regard" to equitable representation of women, minorities, and individuals with disabilities who are involved in the humanities when making appointments to the National Council on the Humanities.

**20 U.S.C. § 959**: Requires the NEA Chairperson to ensure that all advisory panels are composed, to the extent practicable, of individuals reflecting a wide geographic, ethnic, and minority representation, as well as individuals reflecting diverse artistic and cultural points of view.

**20 U.S.C. §§ 1022 et seq.**: Establish the Teacher Quality Partnership Grants program, a stated purpose of which is to recruit highly qualified individuals, including minorities and individuals from other occupations, into the teaching force.

**20 U.S.C. § 1032a**: Authorizes grants, contracts, and cooperative agreements for consortia to carry out projects to develop teaching with modern digital age tools. Eligible consortia must collaborate with educational institutions that teach courses to pre-service teachers so as to better reach underrepresented pre-service teacher populations with programs that connect such populations with applications of technology.

**20 U.S.C. § 1033a**: Authorizes the Secretary of Education to award grants to minority-serving institutions of higher education under the Honorable Augustus F. Hawkins Centers for Excellence to enhance teacher education.

**20 U.S.C. §§ 1051 et seq.**: Provide a range of assistance to institutions of higher education that serve high percentages of minority students.

**20 U.S.C. §§ 1070a-12 et seq.**: Authorize grants under the Federal Trio Programs for various educational programs and services provided to individuals who are "underrepresented, disadvantaged, and/or students of limited English proficiency."

**20 U.S.C. § 1078-11**: Allows loan forgiveness for individuals who are employed full-time as teachers and are from a population underrepresented in the teaching profession, as determined by the Secretary.

**20 U.S.C. § 1101**: Authorizes programs that provide assistance to HSIs.

**20 U.S.C. § 1131**: Authorizes the Secretary to award competitive grants to minority-serving institutions of higher education for purposes of establishing an Institute for International Public Policy so as to enhance the international competitiveness of the United States by increasing the participation of underrepresented populations in the international service.

**20 U.S.C. § 1135b**: Establishes application criteria for graduate assistance programs in "areas of national need." Grant applicants must set forth policies and procedures to assure that, in making fellowship awards, the institution will seek talented students from traditionally underrepresented backgrounds, as determined by the Secretary.

**20 U.S.C. § 1136**: Establishes the Thurgood Marshall Legal Educational Opportunity Program, which provides assistance to secondary school or college students who are minorities or are from low-income families or economically or otherwise disadvantaged backgrounds.

**20 U.S.C. § 1136a**: Authorizes masters degree programs at HBCUs.

**20 U.S.C. § 1136b**: Authorizes masters degree programs at predominantly black institutions.

**20 U.S.C. § 1141**: Establishes the College Access Challenge Grant program, a primary purpose of which is to provide financial aid and support services to students from underrepresented populations so as to increase the number of such students who enter and remain in college.

**20 U.S.C. § 1161b**: Establishes the Mathematics and Science Scholars program. State governors must prioritize the awarding of scholarships under this subsection to particular eligible students, such as students attending schools in high-need local educational agencies; students who are from groups underrepresented in the fields of mathematics, science, and engineering; students served by local educational agencies that do not meet or exceed state standards in mathematics and science; or other high-need students.

**20 U.S.C. § 1161g**: Establishes the Patsy T. Mink Fellowship Program, which provides, through eligible institutions, fellowship awards to assist highly qualified minorities and women in acquiring doctoral or other terminal degrees in academic areas in which such individuals are underrepresented for purposes of entering the professoriate.

**20 U.S.C. §§ 1161n-2, 1161n-3:** Establish grants for cooperative education, which can only be used, among other things, for outreach to potential participants, including underrepresented and nontraditional populations. Model cooperative education programs in the fields of science and mathematics for underrepresented women and minorities are encouraged.

**20 U.S.C. §§ 2324, § 2342**: Establish career and technical education assistance to the states and authorize funds for, among other things, research centers for the recruitment and retention of career and technical education teachers, faculty, counselors, and administrators, including individuals in groups underrepresented in the teaching profession. State plans must describe the recruitment and retention of career and technical education teachers, faculty, and career guidance and academic counselors, including individuals in groups underrepresented in the teaching profession.

**20 U.S.C. § 3412**: Establishes the Special Assistant for Gender Equity within the Department of Education, who shall promote, coordinate, and evaluate gender equity programs, including the dissemination of information, technical assistance, and coordination of research activities.

**20 U.S.C. § 3420**: Establishes the Office of English Language Acquisition, Language Enhancement, and Academic Achievement for Limited English Proficient Students within the Department of Education, the director of which shall coordinate the administration of bilingual education programs and consult with the Secretary concerning policy decisions affecting bilingual education and minority languages affairs.

**20 U.S.C. § 3912**: Requires that NSF funds available for science and engineering education be used to encourage potential students, including underrepresented and underserved populations, to pursue careers in mathematics, science, engineering, and critical foreign languages.

**20 U.S.C. § 3916**: Requires that 15% of NSF funds for science and engineering education be allocated to faculty exchange and other programs involving higher educational institutions with “an enrollment which includes a substantial percentage of students who are members of a minority group, or who are economically or educationally disadvantaged and institutions which demonstrate a commitment to meet the special educational needs of students who are members of a minority group or are economically or educationally disadvantaged.”

**20 U.S.C. § 3919**: Requires the NSF to make every effort to ensure that consideration is given to proposals containing provisions designed to meet the needs of underrepresented and underserved populations when providing financial assistance for science and engineering education.

**20 U.S.C. § 3985**: Requires applicants for partnerships in mathematics, science, and engineering education to provide assurances that consideration is given to programs and activities designed to meet the needs of under-represented and underserved populations.

**20 U.S.C. § 5205(d)**: Requires that no less than 10% of Eisenhower Exchange Fellowship Program funds "shall be available only for participation by individuals who are representative of United States minority populations."

**20 U.S.C. § 5506**: Requires the Administrator of the Environmental Protection Agency (EPA) to provide for wide geographic, cultural, and minority representation in selecting individuals for environmental internships and fellowships.

**20 U.S.C. § 5508**: Requires the Administrator of the EPA to ensure that the Environmental Education Advisory Council and Task Force has members representing the various geographic regions of the country, has minority representation, and includes members whose professional backgrounds include scientific, policy, and other appropriate disciplines.

**20 U.S.C. § 5983**: Authorizes the Secretary to make grants for the development and implementation of seminars on American government and civics for elementary and secondary school teachers and other educators who work with minority and Native American students.

**20 U.S.C. § 6125**: Establishes School-to-Work Opportunities grants for states, which can fund, among other things, development of training and technical support systems for teachers, employers, mentors, counselors, related services personnel, and others that include specialized training and technical support for the counseling and training of women, minorities, and individuals with disabilities for high-skill, high-wage careers in nontraditional employment.

**20 U.S.C. § 6301**: States that the goal of the No Child Left Behind Act is to meet "the educational needs of low-achieving children in our Nation's highest poverty schools, limited English proficient children, migratory children, children with disabilities, Indian children, neglected or delinquent children, and young children in need of reading assistance; [and] clos[e] the gaps between minority and nonminority students, and between disadvantaged children and their more advantaged peers."

**20 U.S.C. § 6494**: Establishes the Close Up fellowship program, applications for which must contain assurances that, in awarding the fellowships to economically disadvantaged students, special consideration shall be given to the participation of those students with special educational needs, including students with disabilities, ethnic minority students, and students with migrant parents.

**20 U.S.C. § 6623(a)(4)**: Authorizes award of subgrants to local educational agencies that develop and implement "initiatives to promote retention of highly qualified teachers and principals, particularly within elementary schools and secondary schools with a high percentage of low-achieving students, including programs that provide ... financial incentives, to principals who have a record of improving the academic achievement of all students, but particularly students from racial and ethnic minority groups, and students with disabilities."

**20 U.S.C. § 6662(c)(10)**: Authorizes the Secretary of Education to award grants to partnership activities involving the engineering, mathematics, or science department of an institution of higher education and a high-need elementary or secondary school that include "training mathematics and science teachers and developing programs to encourage young women and other underrepresented individuals in mathematics and science careers to pursue postsecondary degrees in majors leading to such careers."

**20 U.S.C. §§ 7283 et seq.**: Authorize programs and grants to implement effective gender-equity policies and programs at all educational levels.

**20 U.S.C. § 9105a(b)(3)**: Requires the President of the Museum and Library Services Board to give due regard to equitable representation of women, minorities, and persons with disabilities who are involved with museums and libraries when making appointments to the Board.

**20 U.S.C. § 9579**: Authorizes the Director of the Institute for Education Sciences to establish fellowships in "institutions of higher education (which may include ... historically Black colleges and universities and other institutions of higher education with large numbers of minority students) that support graduate and postdoctoral study on site at the Institute or at the institution of higher education." The Director shall ensure that women and minorities are actively recruited for participation.

**42 U.S.C. § 1862d**: Requires that at least 12% of the amounts appropriated for the Academic Research Facilities Modernization Program shall be reserved for HBCUs and other institutions that enroll a substantial percentage of Black, Hispanic, or Native American students.

## Energy

**42 U.S.C. § 7141**: Authorizes the Secretary of Energy to provide financial assistance in the form of loans to any minority business enterprise "under such rules as he shall prescribe to assist such enterprises in participating fully in research, development, demonstration, and contract activities of the Department to the extent he considers appropriate."

**42 U.S.C. § 7256 note**: Establishes the goal that 5% of the amounts spent by the Department of Energy in carrying out national security programs in each fiscal year between FY1994 and FY2000 were to be spent with SDBs, HBCUs, and minority institutions.

**42 U.S.C. § 7381r**: Establishes a mentoring program to recruit and mentor women and underrepresented minorities interested in careers in science, engineering, and mathematics.

**42 U.S.C. § 13556**: Requires that "[t]o the extent practicable," the head of each agency shall provide that "not less than 10 percent of the total combined amounts obligated for contracts and subcontracts" under the Energy Policy Act of 1992 be expended with socially and economically disadvantaged individuals, women, HBCUs, or college and universities with more than 20% Hispanic or Native American enrollment.

**42 U.S.C. § 16161**: Requires the Secretary to support programs at HBCUs, minority institutions of higher education, and institutions of higher education located in selected states for the development of solar energy technologies and wind energy technologies for the production of hydrogen.

**42 U.S.C. § 16311**: Authorizes $49 million for each of the fiscal years 2005 through 2009 for integrated bioenergy research and development programs, projects, and activities, at least $5 million of which (for each fiscal year) shall be for training and education targeted to minority and socially disadvantaged farmers and ranchers.

**42 U.S.C. § 16534**: Requires the Director of the Office of Science to "endeavor to ensure" that the grant recipients represent various types of institutions of higher education and nonprofit, nondegree-granting research organizations, including minority institutions.

**42 U.S.C. § 17172**: Authorizes grants for solar energy curriculum, which shall be awarded with "[d]ue consideration" given to women, underrepresented minorities, and persons with disabilities.

## Environment

**10 U.S.C. § 2904**: Requires the Secretaries of Defense and Energy, in consultation with the Administrator of the EPA, to jointly appoint a Strategic Environmental Research and Development Program Scientific Advisory Board, whose members shall be appointed with "due regard" given to the equitable representation of scientists and engineers who are women or who represent minority groups.

**42 U.S.C. § 4370d**: Requires the EPA Administrator to ensure that at least 8% of federal funding for prime contracts and subcontracts awarded "in support of authorized programs, including grants, loans, and contracts for wastewater treatment and leaking underground storage tanks grants" be made available to small businesses owned and controlled by socially and economically disadvantaged individuals or HBCUs.

**42 U.S.C. § 7601 note**: Requires that the EPA Administrator, to the extent practicable, ensure that not less than 10% of the total federal funding for research related to the requirements of the Clean Air Act Amendments of 1990 be made available to disadvantaged businesses, HBCUs, or other minority institutions of higher education. Use of quotas or "requirement[s] that [have] the effect of a quota" is prohibited.

## Health and Human Services

**21 U.S.C. § 1177**: Creates special-project grants and contracts for drug abuse prevention, treatment, and rehabilitation. The Secretary of Health and Human Services shall encourage the submission of and give special consideration to applications for programs and projects aimed at underserved populations, such as racial and ethnic minorities, Native Americans, youth, the elderly, women, handicapped individuals, and families of drug abusers.

**42 U.S.C. § 237a, 42 U.S.C. § 242s, 42 U.S.C. § 299b-24a, 42 U.S.C. § 914, 21 U.S.C. § 399b**: Requires the establishment of Offices of Women's Health in each of the Office of the Secretary, Office of the Director of the Centers for Disease Control and Prevention, Office of the Director of Healthcare and Quality Research, Office of the Administrator of the Health Resources and Health Services Administration, and Office of the Commissioner of Food and Drugs. These centers are to establish goals and objectives, identify projects to conduct or support, provide information, and consult with relevant stakeholders in order to improve women's health.

**42 U.S.C. § 247b-5**: Authorizes the Centers for Disease Control and Prevention (CDC) to make grants to states and local health departments to carry out programs that may include the needs of underserved and minority populations regarding prostate cancer.

**42 U.S.C. § 247b-17**: Requires the Secretary to carry out a national campaign to increase health care providers and women's knowledge regarding gynecologic cancers.

**42 U.S.C. § 247c-1**: Authorizes the Director of the CDC to make grants to states, political subdivisions of states, and other public or nonprofit private entities for the purpose of carrying out the activities described in subsection (c) regarding any treatable sexually transmitted disease that can cause infertility in women if treatment is not received.

**42 U.S.C. § 274**: Requires the Organ Procurement and Transplantation Network to carry out studies and demonstration projects for the purpose of improving procedures for organ donation procurement and allocation, including but not limited to projects to examine and attempt to increase transplantation among populations with special needs, including children and individuals who are members of racial or ethnic minority groups.

**42 U.S.C. § 274k**: Authorizes the Secretary, though the Administrator of the Health Resources and Services Administration, to establish, by one or more contracts, a C.W. Bill Young Cell Transplantation Program, which shall carry out a program for the recruitment of bone marrow donors, including increasing the representation of racial and ethnic minority groups (including persons of mixed ancestry) in the program.

**42 U.S.C. § 280c–3**: Directs the Secretary to make grants to states for demonstration projects on Alzheimer's Disease so as improve individuals' access to home-based or community-based longterm care, particularly "individuals who are members of racial or ethnic minority groups, who have limited proficiency in speaking the English language, or who live in rural areas."

**42 U.S.C. § 280m**: Establishes a young women's breast health awareness and support program and requires a public health campaign promoting breast health in young women of all racial, ethnic, and cultural backgrounds.

**42 U.S.C. § 281**: Establishes the National Institute on Minority Health and Health Disparities within the National Institutes of Health (NIH).

**42 U.S.C. § 285a-6**: Directs the National Cancer Institute, in consultation with the National Cancer Advisory Board, to intensify and coordinate the Institute's activities with respect to research on breast and ovarian cancer and other cancers of the reproductive system of women.

**42 U.S.C. § 285b-7a**: Directs the National Heart, Lung, and Blood Institute, to expand, intensify, and coordinate research and related activities with respect to heart attack, stroke, and other cardiovascular diseases in women.

**42 U.S.C. § 285e-10**: Directs the National Institute on Aging, in cooperation with the other national research institutes and agencies of NIH, to conduct research into women's aging processes.

**42 U.S.C. § 287d**: Establishes the Office of Research on Women's Health.

**42 U.S.C. § 288**: Creates the Ruth L. Kirschstein National Research Service Awards for biomedical and behavioral research and provides grant making authority. The Secretary shall carry out the program in a manner that will result in the recruitment of women and individuals from disadvantaged backgrounds, including racial and ethnic minorities, into fields of biomedical or behavior research and in the provision of research training to women and such individuals.

**42 U.S.C. § 289a-2**: Requires the Director of NIH to ensure that women and minority groups are included as subjects when conducting or supporting clinical research.

**42 U.S.C. § 290aa**: Establishes the Associate Administrator for Women's Services within the Substance Abuse and Mental Health Services Administration.

**42 U.S.C. § 292t**: Prohibits the Secretary from making a federal capital contribution to a health professions school to participate in the student loan program unless the school is (1) carrying out a program for recruiting and retaining students from disadvantaged backgrounds, including racial and ethnic minorities, and recruiting and retaining minority faculty; and (2) agrees to: ensure that adequate instruction regarding minority health issues is provided in the school's curricula; enter into arrangements with health clinics providing services to significant numbers of individuals from disadvantaged backgrounds, including minority groups, to provide students with experience in providing clinical services to such individuals; enter into agreements with public or nonprofit private secondary educational institutions and undergraduate institutions of higher education for the purpose of carrying out programs regarding the educational preparation of disadvantaged students, including minority students, to enter the health professions and regarding the recruitment of such individuals into the health professions; and establish a mentor program to assist disadvantaged students, including minority students, in completing the school's educational requirements for degrees. The Secretary shall give special consideration to schools that have enrollments of underrepresented minorities above the national average for health professions schools when making federal capital contributions to student loan funds.

**42 U.S.C. § 293**: Requires the Secretary to make grants to, and enter into contracts with, designated health professions schools and other public and nonprofit health or educational entities for the purpose of assisting the schools in supporting programs of excellence in health professions education for underrepresented minority individuals.

**42 U.S.C. §§ 293a, 293d**: Authorize the Secretary to make grants to eligible entities for the awarding of scholarships for disadvantaged students. The Secretary shall give priority, in awarding grants to eligible entities that are health professions and nursing schools, to eligible entities based on the proportion of graduating students going into primary care, the proportion of underrepresented minority students, and the proportion of graduates working in medically underserved communities.

**42 U.S.C. §§ 293b, § 293d**: Allow the Secretary to make grants to and enter into contracts with eligible entities to assist in increasing the number of underrepresented minority individuals who are members of the faculty of certain eligible schools.

**42 U.S.C. §§ 293c, 293d**: Provide grants for the purpose of assisting individuals from disadvantaged backgrounds, as determined in accordance with criteria prescribed by the Secretary, to undertake education to enter a health profession. The Secretary, to the extent practicable, shall ensure that services and activities are adequately allocated among the various racial and ethnic populations who are from disadvantaged backgrounds.

**42 U.S.C. § 293k**: Requires the Secretary to give priority in awarding grants for the training of interns, residents, or physician assistants, to qualified applicants that have a record of training individuals who are from disadvantaged backgrounds, including racial and ethnic minorities underrepresented among primary care practice or general or pediatric dentistry.

**42 U.S.C. §§ 293l, 294f**: Establish the Advisory Committees on Training in Primary Care Medicine and Dentistry and on Interdisciplinary, Community-Based Linkages. The Secretary shall ensure the adequate representation of women and minorities in appointing the members of the Advisory Committees.

**42 U.S.C. § 295**: Authorizes the Secretary to award grants or contracts to eligible entities to increase the number of individuals in the public health workforce. The Secretary may grant preference to entities serving individuals who are from disadvantaged backgrounds, including underrepresented racial and ethnic minorities.

**42 U.S.C. §§ 296m**: Allows the Secretary to award grants and contracts to eligible entities to meet the costs of special projects intended to increase nursing education opportunities for individuals from disadvantaged backgrounds, including racial and ethnic minorities underrepresented among registered nurses, by providing student scholarships or stipends, pre-entry preparation, and retention activities.

**42 U.S.C. § 297t**: Establishes the National Advisory Council on Nurse Education and Practice and requires the Secretary to ensure adequate representation of minorities in appointing the members of the Council.

**42 U.S.C. § 299a-1**: Directs the Agency for Health Care Research and Quality to conduct and support research and support demonstrations on factors that contribute to health disparities. The Director shall implement research strategies and mechanisms that will enhance the involvement of individuals who are members of minority health disparity populations or other health disparity populations; health services researchers who are such individuals; institutions that train such individuals as researchers; members of minority health disparity populations or other health disparity populations for whom the Agency is attempting to improve the quality and outcomes of care; and representatives of appropriate tribal or other community-based organizations with respect to health disparity populations.

**42 U.S.C. §§ 300k, 300n-4a**: Authorize the Secretary, acting through the Director of the CDC, to make grants to states for the purpose of carrying out programs to screen women for breast and cervical cancer as a preventive health measure.

**42 U.S.C. § 300u-6**: Establishes the Office of Minority Health within the Office of the Secretary to improve minority health and the quality of care received by minorities, as well as eliminate racial and ethnic disparities in health care.

**42 U.S.C. §§ 300x-21, 300x-22, 300x-27**: Establish Center for Substance Abuse Treatment formula grants to states and provide allocation amounts for women.

**42 U.S.C. § 300ee-1**: Directs the Secretary, acting through the Director of the CDC, to establish an office for the purpose of "ensuring that, in carrying out the duties of the Secretary with respect to prevention of acquired immune deficiency syndrome, the Secretary develops and implements prevention programs targeted at minority populations and provides appropriate technical assistance in the implementation of such programs."

**42 U.S.C. § 300ee-34**: Authorizes appropriations for prevention of acquired immune deficiency syndrome national information programs and directs allocations for financial assistance to minority entities for the provision of services to minority populations.

**42 U.S.C. § 300ff-71**: Requires the Secretary, acting through the Administrator of the Health Resources and Services Administration, to award grants to public and nonprofit private entities for the purpose of providing family-centered care involving outpatient or ambulatory care for women, infants, children, and youth with HIV/AIDS.

**42 U.S.C. § 300ff-121**: Directs the Health Resources and Services Administration to develop a formula for awarding certain Minority AIDS Initiative grants "that ensures that funding is provided based on the distribution of populations disproportionately impacted by HIV/AIDS."

**42 U.S.C. § 464z-3**: Establishes the National Center on Minority Health and Health Disparities to conduct and support research, training, dissemination of information, and other programs with respect to minority health conditions and other populations with health disparities. The director of the center shall give priority to conducting and supporting minority health disparities research.

**42 U.S.C. § 464z-4**: Requires the Center on Minority Health and Health Disparities to award grants or contracts to designated biomedical and behavioral research institutions or consortia for the purpose of assisting the institutions in supporting programs of excellence in biomedical and behavioral research training for individuals who are members of minority health disparity populations or other health disparity populations.

**42 U.S.C. § 464z-5**: Establishes a program of contracting with qualified health professionals under which such professionals agree to engage in minority health disparities research or other health disparities research in consideration for the federal government agreeing to repay, for each year of engaging in such research, not more than $35,000 (principal and interest) on their educational loans.

**42 U.S.C. § 673**: Establishes state payments for adoptive parents of children with "special needs," which include specific factors or conditions, such as ethnic background, age, or membership in a minority or sibling group, or the presence of factors such as medical conditions or physical, mental, or emotional handicaps, because of which it is reasonable to conclude that the child cannot be placed with adoptive parents without adoption assistance.

**42 U.S.C. §§ 1397aa et seq.**: Establish grants for outreach programs for racial and ethnic minorities under the State Children's Health Insurance Program.

**42 U.S.C. § 1761**: Encourages "efforts" by service institutions to use small businesses and minority-owned businesses as sources of supplies and services. Such efforts shall afford those firms the maximum feasible opportunity to compete for contracts using program funds.

**42 U.S.C. § 3025**: Requires state agencies to provide assurance that preference in Older Americans programs will be given to providing services to low-income older individuals, including low-income minority older individuals and older individuals with limited English proficiency.

**42 U.S.C. § 3027(a)(20)**: Requires that state plans for grant programs on aging "shall provide assurances that special efforts will be made to provide technical assistance to minority providers of services."

**42 U.S.C. § 3032f**: Authorizes the Assistant Secretary to award grants and contracts to eligible organizations to carry out projects to provide opportunities for older individuals to participate in multigenerational activities and civic engagement. The Assistant Secretary shall give preference to eligible organizations proposing multigenerational activity projects that will serve older individuals and communities with the greatest need, with particular attention to low-income minority individuals, older individuals with limited English proficiency, older individuals residing in rural areas, and low-income minority communities.

**42 U.S.C. § 3056**: Establishes caps for administrative expenses under a community services program for older Americans, but authorizes the Secretary to increase the amount available to pay administrative costs if a grantee demonstrates that the number of eligible minority individuals participating in the project will decline if the amount available to pay administrative costs is increased.

**42 U.S.C. § 5023**: Requires the Director to take appropriate steps to ensure that special efforts are made to recruit, select, and assign qualified individuals age 55 years or older from minority populations to serve as volunteers under National Senior Service Corps.

**42 U.S.C. § 5113**: Directs the Secretary to provide for the provision of technical assistance in planning, improving, developing, and carrying out programs and activities relating to adoption and promote professional leadership training of minorities in the adoption field.

**42 U.S.C. § 5116d**: Requires community-based application grants for the prevention of child abuse and neglect to include a description of outreach activities that will be undertaken to "maximize the participation of racial and ethnic minorities, children and adults with disabilities, homeless families and those at risk of homelessness, and members of other underserved or underrepresented groups" by the grant recipient and any community-based and prevention-focused programs and activities designed to strengthen and support families to prevent child abuse and neglect.

**42 U.S.C. § 9843**: Authorizes Head Start technical assistance and training grants for HBCUs, HSIs, and tribal colleges and universities to, among other things, develop program curricula to promote high-quality services and instruction to children with diverse backgrounds, including African American, Hispanic, and Indian children.

**42 U.S.C. § 10410**: Provides grants for states for funding of state domestic violence coalitions that further the purposes of domestic violence intervention and prevention activities. Such activities include conducting public education campaigns regarding domestic violence through the use of public service announcements and informative materials that are designed for print media, billboards, public transit advertising, electronic broadcast media, and other vehicles for information that inform the public about domestic violence, including information aimed at underserved racial, ethnic or language-minority populations.

**42 U.S.C. § 11225**: Establishes the National Alzheimer's Project within the Office of the Secretary, which is to ensure the inclusion of ethnic and racial populations at higher risk of

Alzheimer's, or less likely to receive care, in clinical, research, and service efforts with the purpose of decreasing health disparities in Alzheimer's.

**42 U.S.C. §§ 13925 et seq.**: Establish the Violence Against Women Act and authorize several grant programs aimed at preventing violence against women.

**42 U.S.C. § 15024**: Requires that state plans for federal assistance to state councils on developmental disabilities include assurances that the state has taken affirmative steps to assure that participation in funded programs is geographically representative of the state and reflects the state's diversity with respect to race and ethnicity.

## Homeland Security

**6 U.S.C. § 195c**: Requires the Director of the Science and Technology Homeland Security International Cooperative Programs Office at the Department of Homeland Security (DHS) to facilitate the planning, development, and implementation of international cooperative activity through grants, cooperative agreements, or contracts with foreign public or private entities; governmental organizations; businesses, including small businesses and socially and economically disadvantaged small businesses; federally funded research and development centers; and universities.

**6 U.S.C. § 321m**: Establishes a voluntary private sector preparedness accreditation and certification program and provides that, in accrediting qualified third parties to carry out the certification process under this subsection, selected entities shall ensure, to the extent practicable, that the third parties include qualified small, minority, women-owned, or disadvantaged business concerns when appropriate.

**6 U.S.C. § 415**: Establishes the Homeland Security Education Program and requires the Administrator to take reasonable steps to ensure that the student body represents racial, gender, and ethnic diversity.

**6 U.S.C. 592**: Establishes the National Nuclear Forensics Expertise Development Program and directs it to encourage the participation of students and faculty from HBCUs, Hispanic-serving institutions, Tribal Colleges and Universities, Asian American and Native American Pacific Islander-serving institutions, Alaska Native-serving institutions, and Hawaiian Native-serving institutions when awarding undergraduate scholarships, graduate fellowships, and faculty awards for study in nuclear and geochemical science specialties directly relevant to technical nuclear forensics.

**6 U.S.C. § 1135**: Requires that the Secretary of Homeland Security issue guidelines to ensure that eligible public transportation agencies receiving grants for security improvements use minority or disadvantaged concerns "to the extent possible."

**6 U.S.C. § 1152**: Directs the Secretary to ensure, to the extent practicable, that Amtrak grant recipients under this title who use contractors or subcontractors use small, minority, women-owned, or disadvantaged business concerns as contractors or subcontractors when appropriate.

**15 U.S.C. § 2229a**: Establishes grant making authority for the U.S. Fire Service and requires grant applications to provide, at a minimum, assurances that the applicant will, to the extent practicable, seek, recruit, and hire members of racial and ethnic minority groups and women in order to increase their ranks within firefighting.

**42 U.S.C. § 5197h**: Establishes the minority emergency preparedness demonstration program, which provides for grants, contracts, or cooperative agreements with eligible organizations, including nonprofits whose primary mission is to provide services to communities predominately populated by minority citizens and that can demonstrate partnerships with minority-owned businesses or minority businesses located in HUBZones.

## Housing and Urban Development

**12 U.S.C. § 1701q**: Directs the Secretary of Housing and Urban Development to make available appropriate technical assistance to assure that applicants having limited resources, particularly minority applicants, are able to participate more fully in the supportive housing for the elderly program.

**12 U.S.C. § 4108**: Authorizes the Secretary to approve a plan of action that provides for termination of the low-income affordability restrictions through prepayment of the mortgage or voluntary termination of the mortgage insurance contract only upon a written finding that the supply of vacant, comparable housing is sufficient to ensure that such prepayment will not materially affect the housing opportunities of minorities in the community within which the housing is located.

**12 U.S.C. § 4565**: Requires government-sponsored enterprises to take affirmative steps to assist primary lenders to make housing credit available in areas with concentrations of low-income and minority families.

**42 U.S.C. §§ 3025 et seq.**: Require state agencies to provide assurance that preference will be given to providing services to older individuals with the greatest economic and social need, with particular attention to low-income older individuals, including low-income minority older individuals, older individuals with limited English proficiency, and older individuals residing in rural areas.

**42 U.S.C. § 5307**: Authorizes the Secretary to make grants to HBCUs to expand their role and effectiveness in addressing community development needs, including neighborhood revitalization, housing, and economic development in their localities.

**42 U.S.C. § 12831**: Requires each participating jurisdiction to prescribe procedures acceptable to the Secretary to establish and oversee a minority outreach program within that jurisdiction to ensure the inclusion, to the maximum extent possible, of minorities, women, and entities owned by minorities and women, including real estate firms, construction firms, appraisal firms, management firms, financial institutions, investment banking firms, underwriters, accountants, and providers of legal services, in all contracts entered into by the participating jurisdiction so as to facilitate the jurisdiction's efforts to provide affordable housing authorized under this act or other applicable federal housing law.

## Immigration and Naturalization

**8 U.S.C. § 1522(a)(1)(A):** Requires the Director to (1) make available sufficient resources for employment training and placement in order to achieve economic self-sufficiency among refugees as quickly as possible; (2) provide refugees with the opportunity to acquire sufficient English language training to enable them to become effectively resettled as quickly as possible; (3) ensure that cash assistance is made available to refugees in such a manner as not to discourage their economic self-sufficiency; and (4) ensure that women have the same opportunities as men to participate in training and instruction.

## Interior

**16 U.S.C. § 470a**: Authorizes the Secretary of Interior to make grants or loans to "nonprofit organizations representing ethnic or minority groups" for the preservation of their cultural heritage.

**16 U.S.C. § 590h**: Establishes state, county, and area committees on conservation and environmental assistance and requires the Secretary to solicit and accept nominations from organizations representing the interests of socially disadvantaged groups.

**16 U.S.C. § 1445c**: Requires the Secretary to establish and administer through the National Ocean Service the Dr. Nancy Foster Scholarship Program to provide graduate education scholarships in oceanography, marine biology or maritime archeology, particularly to members of minority groups.

**16 U.S.C. § 1649**: Establishes the Forestry Student Grant Program to provide assistance to expand the professional education of forestry, natural resources, and environmental scientists.

The program includes competitive grant fellowships to assist undergraduate and graduate minority or female students attending institutions having programs in forestry and natural resources.

**16 U.S.C. § 1725**: Authorizes the Secretary to provide "resource assistants" to any federal land managing agency, with preference in the selection of assistants being given to individuals who are enrolled in an institution of higher education or are recent graduates from an institution of higher education, particularly women and participants from historically black, Hispanic, and Native American schools.

**16 U.S.C. § 2504**: Establishes federal assistance grants for the Urban Park and Recreation Recovery Program.

Criteria for project selection and approval include the extent to which a proposed project would provide employment opportunities for minorities, youth, and low- and moderate-income residents in the project neighborhood.

## Internal Revenue

**26 U.S.C. § 36C**: Details allowances for qualified adoption expenses, including for "children with special needs," or children who have specific factors or conditions, such as their ethnic background, age, or membership in a minority or sibling group, medical conditions or physical, mental, or emotional handicaps, which make it reasonable to conclude that they cannot be placed with adoptive parents without providing adoption assistance.

## Justice

**31 U.S.C. § 3718**: Requires the Attorney General to use his or her "best efforts" when entering into contracts with law firms owned and controlled by socially and economically disadvantaged individuals when retaining private counsel to furnish legal services in the case of claims of indebtedness owed to the United States.

**31 U.S.C. § 6701(f)**: Requires that not less than 10% of the amount paid from the Local Government Fiscal Assistance Fund created by the Violent Crime Control Act be expended on contracts or subcontracts with socially and economically disadvantaged small businesses, WOSBs, HBCUs, and institutions of higher education with more than 20% Hispanic or Native-American student enrollment.

**42 U.S.C. § 3796dd-1**: Establishes the "Cops on the Beat" program. Applicants must provide assurances that they will, to the extent practicable, seek, recruit, and hire members of racial and ethnic minority groups and women in order to increase their ranks within the sworn positions in the law enforcement agency.

**42 U.S.C. §§ 3796gg et seq.**: Establish a program of grants to states to provide personnel, training, technical assistance, data collection and other equipment for the more widespread apprehension, prosecution, and adjudication of persons committing violent crimes against women, as well as the Violence Against Women Office.

## Labor

**15 U.S.C. § 1022a**: Requires the President to incorporate medium-term annual numerical goals in each Economic Report in order to reduce unemployment and directs that every effort shall be made to reduce differences between the rates of unemployment among youth, women, minorities, handicapped persons, veterans, middle-aged and older persons and other labor force groups and the overall rate of unemployment which are caused by any improper factors with the ultimate objective of removing such differentials to the extent possible.

**29 U.S.C. §§ 11 et seq.**: Establish Women's Bureau of the Department of Labor, which has the duty of formulating standards and policies that promote the welfare of wage-earning women, improve their working condition, increase their efficiency, and advance their opportunities for profitable employment and which has the authority to investigate and report to the Department of Labor upon all matters pertaining to the welfare of women in industry.

**29 U.S.C. § 718**: Requires the Commissioner and Director to require entities receiving funding for rehabilitation services under grants, contracts, or cooperative agreements to demonstrate how they will address, in whole or in part, the needs of individuals with disabilities from minority backgrounds.

**29 U.S.C. §§ 2503-2504**: Require the Secretary of Labor to give priority in awarding grants for women in apprenticeship and nontraditional occupations to applications from community-based organizations that demonstrate experience preparing women to gain employment in apprenticeable occupations or other nontraditional occupations; demonstrate experience working with the business community to prepare them to place women in apprenticeable occupations or other nontraditional occupations; have tradeswomen or women in nontraditional occupations as active members of the organization, as either employed staff or board members; and have experience delivering technical assistance.

**29 U.S.C. § 2918a**: Establishes the YouthBuild Program and requires the Secretary to ensure that grant applications contain, at a minimum, descriptions of the special outreach efforts that will be undertaken to recruit eligible young women, including young women with dependent children, as participants.

## Office of Personnel Management

**5 U.S.C. § 4107(b)**: Requires agencies to, consistent with merit systems principles, take into consideration the need to maintain a balanced workforce in which women, members of racial and ethnic minority groups, and persons with disabilities are appropriately represented in government service when exercising authority to select and assign an employee to academic degree training.

**5 U.S.C. § 4313**: Requires appraisals of performance in the Senior Executive Service to be based on both individual and organizational performance, taking into account such factors as meeting affirmative action goals, achievement of equal employment opportunity requirements, and compliance with the merit systems principles.

**5 U.S.C. § 5379(e)**: Requires agencies to, consistent with the merit system principles, take into consideration the need to maintain a balanced workforce in which women and members of racial and ethnic minority groups are appropriately represented in government service when selecting employees to receive student loan repayment benefits.

**5 U.S.C. § 7201**: Describes the federal government's antidiscrimination policy and minority recruitment program and specifies that it is the policy of the United States to ensure equal employment opportunities for employees without discrimination because of race, color, religion, sex, or national origin. Each executive agency must also conduct a continuing program for the recruitment of members of minorities to eliminate "underrepresentation" of minorities in the various categories of civil service employment within the federal service.

**5 U.S.C. § 8473(b)**: Requires the Chairman of the 25-member Employee Thrift Advisory Council to appoint one member to represent employee organizations having as a purpose promoting the interests of women in government service.

**31 U.S.C. § 732**: Requires the personnel management system include a minority recruitment program.

## Science and Technology

**15 U.S.C. § 278g-1, 278g-2**: Require the director of the National Institute of Standards and Technology to give consideration to the goal of promoting the participation of underrepresented minorities in research areas supported by the institute when evaluating applications for research and postdoctoral fellowships. Applications from teachers from high-need schools are also to be given special consideration in selecting participants for the teacher development program.

**15 U.S.C. § 1542**: Establishes the Ernest F. Hollings Scholarship Program, which shall promote participation by groups underrepresented in oceanic and atmospheric science and technology.

**33 U.S.C. §§ 893a, 1127**: Establish the National Sea Grant College Program and require the Administrator of the National Oceanic and Atmospheric Administration (NOAA) to allocate funding among sea grant colleges and institutes so as to encourage cooperation with minority-serving institutions to enhance collaborative research opportunities and increase the number of such students graduating in NOAA science areas. The Secretary of Commerce shall strive to ensure equal access for minority and economically disadvantaged students to the program carried out under this subsection.

**42 U.S.C. § 1862n-1**: Establishes the Robert Noyce Teacher Scholarship Program and requires the Director to broadly disseminate information about when and how to apply for grants under this section, including by conducting outreach to HBCUs and minority institutions.

**42 U.S.C. § 1862n-10**: Authorizes the Director of the NSF to establish a program to award competitive, merit-based grants to HSIs, ANNHIs, and other institutions of higher education serving a substantial number of minority students to enhance the quality of undergraduate science, mathematics, and engineering education at such institutions and to increase the retention and graduation rates of students pursuing associate's or baccalaureate degrees in science, mathematics, engineering, or technology.

**42 U.S.C. § 1863**: Establishes the National Science Board and requires the President to give due regard to equitable representation of scientists and engineers who are women or who represent minority groups when making nominations to the Board.

**42 U.S.C. § 1885a**: Authorizes the NSF to support activities designed to increase the participation of women in courses of study at the undergraduate, graduate, and postgraduate levels leading to degrees in scientific and engineering fields; encourage women to consider and prepare for careers in science and engineering; or provide traineeship and fellowship opportunities for women in science and engineering.

**42 U.S.C. § 1885c**: Establishes the Committee on Equal Opportunities in Science and Engineering, which is responsible for reviewing and evaluating all NSF matters relating to opportunities for the participation in, and the advancement of, women, minorities, and persons with disabilities in education, training, and science and engineering research programs.

**51 U.S.C. § 30304**: Requires the NASA Administrator to annually establish as a goal that at least 8% of the total value of prime contracts and subcontracts awarded in support of authorized programs be made to small businesses or other organizations owned or controlled by socially and economically disadvantaged individuals, including HBCUs, HSIs, ANNHIs, tribal colleges or universities, and minority educational institutions.

**51 U.S.C. § 30305**: Requires NASA to competitively select organizations to partner with NASA centers, aerospace contractors, and academic institutions to carry out a program to help promote the competitiveness of small, minority-owned, and women-owned businesses through enhanced insight into the technologies of NASA's space and aeronautics programs.

**51 U.S.C. § 40906**: Encourages the NASA Administrator to ensure equal access for minority and economically disadvantaged students to NASA's education programs and requires the Administrator to establish the Dr. Mae C. Jemison Grant Program to work with minority serving institutions to bring more women of color into the field of space and aeronautics.

## Small Business

**15 U.S.C. § 631**: Establishes the Minority Small Business and Capital Development Program, commonly known as the 8(a) Program and described among the government-wide programs, which is intended to (1) promote the business development of small business concerns owned and controlled by socially and economically disadvantaged individuals so that such concerns can compete on an equal basis in the American economy; (2) promote the competitive viability of such concerns in the marketplace by providing such available contract, financial, technical, and management assistance as may be necessary; and (3) increase procurement of articles, supplies, services, materials, and construction work from small business concerns owned by socially and economically disadvantaged individuals.

**15 U.S.C. § 633**: Creates an Associate Administrator for Minority Small Business and Capital Ownership Development, who shall be an employee in the competitive service or in the Senior Executive Service and a career appointee and shall be responsible to the SBA Administrator for the formulation and execution of the policies and programs under certain sections of the Small Business Act that provide assistance to minority small business concerns.

**15 U.S.C. § 634b**: Establishes the Office of Advocacy, whose functions include evaluating the efforts of Federal agencies, business, and industry to assist minority enterprises and making such other recommendations as may be appropriate to assist the development and strengthening of minority and other small business enterprises.

**15 U.S.C. § 636(m)**: Establishes the SBA's "microloan program," under which it can make direct loans to "eligible intermediaries" to enable such intermediaries to make "small-scale loans, particularly loans in amounts averaging not more than $10,000," to start-up, newly established, or growing small business concerns owned by women and minorities, among others, for working capital or the acquisition of materials, supplies, or equipment.

**15 U.S.C. § 648**: Authorizes the SBA to make grants to assist in establishing small business development centers. Grants may be used solely to assist with outreach, development, and enhancement of minority-owned small business startups or expansions, HUBZone small business concerns, veteran-owned small business startups or expansions, and WOSB startups or expansions, in communities impacted by base closings or military or corporate downsizing, or in rural or underserved communities.

**15 U.S.C. § 656**: Establishes the Women's Business Center Program, under which the SBA may provide financial assistance to private nonprofit organizations to conduct five-year projects for the benefit of WOSBs.

**15 U.S.C. § 657d**: Establishes the Federal and State Technology (FAST) Partnership Program, with the purpose of strengthening the technological competitiveness of small businesses. The SBA Administrator and the SBIR program managers at the NSF and DOD may consider whether the proposal addresses the needs of WOSBs and small businesses owned and controlled by minorities when making awards or entering into cooperative agreements.

**15 U.S.C. § 694b**: Establishes the SBA surety bond guarantees program and grants the SBA authority to pay up to 90% of the losses incurred by sureties from breach of the terms of a bid, payment, performance or other bond of a SDB or HUBZone small business that did not exceed $5 million at the time the bond was executed if the SBA specifically approved issuance of the bond.

**15 U.S.C. § 695**: Authorizes loans to foster economic development through the state development company program, which funds projects directed toward at least one of several development objectives, one of which is the development of minority- or women-owned businesses.

## State Department and Foreign Affairs

**22 U.S.C. § 2151 note**: Gives the Minority Resource Center responsibility for increasing the participation of economically and socially disadvantaged business enterprises in contract, procurement, grant, and research and development activities funded under Part I of the Foreign Assistance Act of 1961. Among other things, the Center shall (1) serve as a clearinghouse for information; (2) design programs; (3) conduct market research; and (4) develop support mechanisms for such firms.

**22 U.S.C. § 2665a**: Requires that "priority consideration" for Foreign Service fellowships be given to higher education faculty members who teach in programs in international affairs that serve significant numbers of students from cultural and ethnic groups underrepresented in the Foreign Service.

**22 U.S.C. § 2719**: Requires the Secretary of State to give special emphasis to promoting knowledge and awareness of, and interest in employment with, the Foreign Service among minority students.

**22 U.S.C. § 3905**: Establishes a minority recruitment program for the Foreign Service.

**22 U.S.C. § 3922a**: Requires the head of each agency utilizing the Foreign Service personnel system to develop a plan to significantly increase the number of members of minority groups and women in the Foreign Service in that agency, with particular emphasis on mid-level positions.

**22 U.S.C. § 4002**: Requires the Secretary to assure that substantial number of women and members of minority groups are appointed to each selection board that evaluates the performance of members of the Senior Foreign Service and members of the Service.

**22 U.S.C. § 4852**: Requires that not less than 10% of the amount appropriated for diplomatic construction or design projects each fiscal year be allocated "to the extent practicable" for contracts with U.S. minority contractors.

**22 U.S.C. § 4864(e)**: Requires that not less than 10% of the amount of funds obligated for local guard contracts for Foreign Service buildings be allocated "to the extent practicable" for contracts with minority small business contractors.

**22 U.S.C. § 6102**: Requires the Mansfield Center for Pacific Affairs to select Mansfield Fellowship recipients based solely on merit and make positive efforts to recruit candidates reflecting the cultural, racial, and ethnic diversity of the United States.

## Transportation

**23 U.S.C. § 101 note**: Requires that not less than 10% of the amounts made available in federal highway funds under Titles I, III, and V of P.L. 109-59 or under 23 U.S.C. § 403 be expended through disadvantaged business enterprises (DBEs). States are required to survey and compile an annual listing of DBEs within the state and notify the Secretary of Transportation in writing of the percentage of various types of such firms.

**23 U.S.C. § 504(d)**: Establishes the Dwight David Eisenhower Transportation Fellowship Program and Garrett Morgan Technology and Education Program to provide grants to education agencies, with a priority for programs targeting minorities and women.

**49 U.S.C. § 332**: Establishes the Minority Resource Center within the Department of Transportation.

**49 U.S.C. § 5322**: Authorizes the Secretary to undertake, or make grants and contracts for, programs that address human resource needs as they apply to public transportation activities, including outreach program to increase minority and female employment in public transportation activities and training and assistance for minority business opportunities.

**49 U.S.C. § 40110**: Authorizes the head of the Federal Aviation Administration (FAA) to develop and implement an acquisition management system that addresses the unique needs of the agency. Certain provisions of federal law, including the Small Business Act, do not apply to this system. However, small businesses and small businesses owned and controlled by socially and economically disadvantaged individuals shall nonetheless be given "all reasonable opportunities to be awarded contracts."

**49 U.S.C. § 44511**: Establishes aviation research grants and requires the Administrator to establish a solicitation, review, and evaluation process that ensures the inclusion of historically black institutions of higher education and other minority nonprofit research organizations.

**49 U.S.C. § 47107**: Authorizes the Secretary to approve project grant applications for airport development projects only if there are satisfactory written assurances that the airport owner or operator will take any actions necessary to ensure, "to the maximum extent practicable," that at least 10% of all businesses selling consumer products or providing consumer services at the airport are owned and controlled by DBEs.

## Veterans Affairs

**38 U.S.C. §§ 317, 318**: Establish Centers for Minority and Women Veterans.

**38 U.S.C. §§ 542, 544**: Establish Advisory Committees on Minority and Women Veterans.

**38 U.S.C. § 1712a**: Establishes a pilot program to evaluate the feasibility and advisability of providing reintegration and readjustment services (including financial and occupational counseling and information and counseling on stress reduction and conflict resolution) in group retreat settings to women veterans who are recently separated from service in the Armed Forces after prolonged deployment.

**38 U.S.C. § 2021a**: Authorizes grants for programs and facilities that provide dedicated services to homeless women veterans. Grants may be used to provide job training, counseling, placement services, and child care services to expedite the reintegration of homeless women veterans into the labor force.

**38 U.S.C. § 2061**: Establishes a grant program for homeless veterans with special needs, including homeless veterans who are women or women caring for minor dependents.

**38 U.S.C. § 7303**: Authorizes the Department of Veterans Affairs to provide grants to medical research programs that conduct and support clinical research on minorities who are veterans.

## End Notes

[1] The search included all variants of the following words or phrases: underrepresented, affirmative action, minority, woman, disadvantage, race, and gender. Title 25 of the *United States Code*, which focuses upon Native Americans, was deliberately excluded from this search for reasons discussed below. Included are codified statutes that have not been repealed even if the programs they authorized were of limited duration. However, this report does not include statutes that have been repealed, nor does it track appropriations or appropriations riders that could limit the applicability of any of these provisions. There have been instances where failure to appropriate funds or the terms of an appropriations rider effectively render a program inoperative. *See, e.g.*, Strom Thurmond National Defense Authorization Act for FY1999, P.L. 105-261, § 801, 112 Stat. 1921, 2080-81 (Oct. 17, 1998) (barring the Department of Defense (DOD) from exercising its authority under 10 U.S.C. § 2323 to make price evaluation adjustments to the offers of small disadvantaged businesses (SDBs) in any fiscal year directly following a fiscal year in which DOD awarded at least 5% of its contract dollars to SDBs). This provision kept DOD from granting price evaluation adjustments in every fiscal year between 1998 and 2009. *See* Rothe Dev. Corp. v. Dep't of Defense, 545 F.3d 1023, 1028 (Fed. Cir. 2008) (addressing DOD's authority in

fiscal years 1998 to 2007); 48 C.F.R. Subpart 19.11 (2008) (suspending price evaluation adjustment authority for FY2008); Dep't of Defense, Suspension of the Price Evaluation Adjustment for Small Disadvantaged Businesses, 74 Fed. Reg. 7671 (Feb. 19, 2009) (suspending price evaluation adjustment authority for FY2009).

[2] The word "disadvantaged" commonly appears in federal and federally funded contracting programs. Many programs, especially those for small businesses, include a presumption that members of certain racial or ethnic groups, or women, are socially and/or economically disadvantaged. *See* CRS Report R40987, *"Disadvantaged" Small Businesses: Definitions and Designations for Purposes of Federal and Federally Funded Contracting Programs*, by Kate M. Manuel. Such presumptions based on race have been found to constitute "explicit racial classifications" and are thus included here. *See* Rothe Dev. Corp., 545 F.3d at 1035.

[3] *See, e.g.*, 15 C.F.R. § 15.3(b)(6)(2003) (Department of Agriculture Title VI regulations).

[4] 42 U.S.C. § 2000e-5(g); 42 U.S.C. § 3613.

[5] Morton v. Mancari, 417 U.S. 535, 548 (1973).

[6] *Id.* at 554.

[7] These programs are largely, even if not entirely, the same as those for Alaska Native Corporations, described in CRS Report R40855, *Contracting Programs for Alaska Native Corporations: Historical Development and Legal Authorities*, by Kate M. Manuel, John R. Luckey, and Jane M. Smith.

[8] *See, e.g.*, 12 U.S.C. § 1723a(n) (requiring reports on, among other things, the volume of mortgages purchased from minority-owned lenders and "any efforts to facilitate relationships with such lenders").

[9] For additional information on minority preferences and affirmative action, see the following CRS reports: CRS Report RS22256, *Federal Affirmative Action Law: A Brief History*, by Jody Feder; CRS Report RL30470, *Affirmative Action in Employment: A Legal Overview*, by Jody Feder; CRS Report RL30410, *Affirmative Action and Diversity in Public Education: Legal Developments*, by Jody Feder; CRS Report RL33284, *Minority Contracting and Affirmative Action for Disadvantaged Small Businesses: Legal Issues*, by Jody Feder; and CRS Report R40744, *The "8(a) Program" for Small Businesses Owned and Controlled by the Socially and Economically Disadvantaged: Legal Requirements and Issues*, by John R. Luckey and Kate M. Manuel.

[10] Agencies conducting negotiated procurements under the authority of the Armed Services Procurement Act of 1947 (10 U.S.C. §§ 2302 et seq.) or the Federal Property and Administrative Services Act of 1949 (40 U.S.C. §§ 471 et seq. and 41 U.S.C. §§ 251 et seq.) could potentially use firms' small business status—including their status as SDBs, women-owned small businesses, or 8(a) firms—as evaluation factors in determining which offer provides "best value" for the government. The relevant statutes do not specifically contemplate agencies' use of these authorities to award contracts to minority- or women-owned firms. However, at least some agencies appear to use them to favor other classes of small businesses. *See* CRS Report R40998, *The Inapplicability of Limitations on Subcontracting to "Preference Contracts" for Small Businesses: Washington-Harris Group*, by Kate M. Manuel.

[11] 48 C.F.R. § 52.222-23(b).

[12] 15 U.S.C. § 644(g)(1).

[13] 15 U.S.C. § 644(g)(2). *See also* Small Business Goaling Report: Fiscal Year 2009, *available at* https://www.fpds.gov/downloads/top_requests/FPDSNG_SB_Goaling_FY_2009.pdf (reporting on agencies' performance in meeting the goals for contracting and subcontracting with small businesses).

[14] 13 C.F.R. § 124.520(a). For more information about the 8(a) Mentor-Protégé Program, see CRS Report R41722, *Small Business Mentor-Protégé Programs*, by Robert Jay Dilger and Kate M. Manuel.

[15] For more on SBIR, see CRS Report 96-402, *Small Business Innovation Research (SBIR) Program*, by Wendy H. Schacht.

[16] 15 U.S.C. § 637(d)(3)(A).

[17] 15 U.S.C. § 637(d)(6)(C).

[18] 15 U.S.C. § 637(d)(4)(B)(iv).

[19] 48 C.F.R. § 19.705-7.

[20] 48 C.F.R. § 42.1502(g).

[21] 15 U.S.C. § 637(m).

[22] 15 U.S.C. § 637(m)(2)(A)-(F) & (m)(4). Implementation of set-asides for women-owned small businesses did not occur until February 2011, in part, because of concerns over the limited number and nature of the industries in which the SBA had found that WOSBs were underrepresented. *See* Small Business Administration, Proposed Rule: Women-Owned Small Business Federal Contract Assistance Procedures, 72 Fed. Reg. 73285 (Dec. 27, 2007) (identifying only four industries in which WOSBs are underrepresented); Robert Brodsky, SBA Issues New Proposal on Small Business Program, But Same Questions Remain, *Gov't Exec.*, Sept. 30, 2008, *available at* http://www.govexec.com/dailyfed/0908/093008rb1.htm (reporting an SBA proposal to increase the number of industries in which women are underrepresented from 4 to 31); Omnibus Appropriations Act, 2009, P.L. 111-8, Administrative Provisions—Small Business Administration, § 522, 123 Stat. 673 (Mar. 11, 2009) (prohibiting SBA from using funds appropriated under the act to implement the set-aside program with the previously identified industries). However, on October 7, 2010, the SBA issued new regulations for the WOSB set-aside program, identifying 83 industries in which women are underrepresented or substantially underrepresented. Small Business Administration, Women-Owned Small Business Federal Contract Program: Final Rule, 75 Fed. Reg. 62258 (Oct. 7, 2010).

[23] Located within the Office of Management and Budget, OFPP provides overall direction of government-wide procurement policies, regulations, procedures, and forms for executive-branch agencies.

[24] 41 U.S.C. § 405(d)(11).

[25] Other agencies had similar authority to make noncompetitive awards or grant price evaluation adjustments to SDBs under the Federal Acquisition Streamlining Act (FASA) of 1994, but this authority expired on September 30, 2003. P.L. 103-355, § 7102, 108 Stat. 3368-69 (Oct. 13, 1994). Agencies' authority under FASA was originally set to expire on September 30, 2000, but it was extended once through September 30, 2003, at which time it was not renewed. *See* 15 U.S.C. § 644 note.

[26] Rothe Dev. Corp., 545 F.3d 1023. For more on the *Rothe* case, see CRS Report R40440, *Rothe Development Corporation v. Department of Defense: The Constitutionality of Federal Contracting Programs for Minority-Owned and Other Small Businesses*, by Jody Feder and Kate M. Manuel.

[27] *See* Rothe Dev. Corp. v. Dep't of Defense, 606 F. Supp. 2d 648, 653 (W.D. Tex. 2009). Even prior to *Rothe*, the Department of Defense was prohibited from making price evaluation adjustments to the offers of SDBs by Section 801 of the Strom Thurmond National Defense Authorization Act for FY1999. *See supra* note 1.

[28] National Defense Authorization Act for FY2010, P.L. 111-84, § 252, 123 Stat. 2242-43 (Oct. 28, 2009) (codified at 10 U.S.C. § 2362).

In: Affirmative Action and Preferential Treatment ISBN: 978-1-62257-465-0
Editors: P. L. Medina and J. E. Patel 

*Chapter 2*

# FEDERAL AFFIRMATIVE ACTION LAW: A BRIEF HISTORY[*]

*Jody Feder*

## SUMMARY

Affirmative action remains a subject of public debate as the result of legal and political developments at the federal, state, and local levels. In recent years, federal courts have reviewed minority admissions programs to state universities; scrutinized the constitutional status of racial diversity policies in public elementary and secondary schools; ruled on minority preferences in public and private employment as a remedy for violation of civil and constitutional rights; and considered federal, state, and local efforts to increase minority participation as contractors and subcontractors on publicly financed construction projects. This report provides a brief history of federal affirmative action law.

The origins of affirmative action law may be traced to the early 1960s as first the Warren, and then the Burger, Court grappled with the seemingly intractable problem of racial segregation in the nation's public schools. Judicial rulings from this period recognized an "affirmative duty," cast upon local school boards by the Equal Protection Clause, to desegregate formerly

[*] This is an edited, reformatted and augmented version of Congressional Research Service, Publication No. RS22256, dated March 11, 2009.

"dual school" systems and to eliminate "root and branch" the last "vestiges" of state-enforced segregation.[1] These holdings ushered in a two decade era of "massive" desegregation— first in the South, and later the urban North— marked by federal desegregation orders frequently requiring drastic reconfiguration of school attendance patterns along racial lines and extensive student transportation schemes. School districts across the nation operating under these decrees later sought to be declared in compliance with constitutional requirements in order to gain release from federal intervention. The Supreme Court eventually responded by holding that judicial control of a school system previously found guilty of intentional segregation should be relinquished if, looking to all aspects of school operations, it appears that the district has complied with desegregation requirements in "good faith" for a "reasonable period of time" and has eliminated "vestiges" of past discrimination "to the extent practicable."[2]

Following the Court's lead, Congress and the Executive approved a panoply of laws and regulations authorizing, either directly or by judicial or administrative interpretation, "race-conscious" strategies to promote minority opportunity in jobs, education, and governmental contracting. The basic statutory framework for affirmative action in employment and education derives from the Civil Rights Act of 1964. Public and private employers with 15 or more employees are subject to a comprehensive code of equal employment opportunity regulations under Title VII of the 1964 Act.[3] The Title VII remedial scheme rests largely on judicial power to order monetary damages and injunctive relief, including "such affirmative action as may be appropriate," to make discrimination victims whole. Except as may be imposed by court order or consent decree to remedy past discrimination, however, there is no general statutory obligation on employers to adopt affirmative action remedies. Official approval of "affirmative action" remedies was further codified by federal regulations construing the 1964 Act's Title VI, which prohibits racial or ethnic discrimination in all federally assisted "programs" and activities,[4] including public or private educational institutions. The Office of Civil Rights of the Department of Education interpreted Title VI to require schools and colleges to take affirmative action to overcome the effects of past discrimination and to encourage affirmative action "[e]ven in the absence of past discrimination ... to overcome the effects of conditions which resulted in limiting participation by persons of a particular race, color, or national origin."[5]

Since the early 1960s, minority participation "goals" have also been integral to Executive Branch enforcement of minority hiring and employment standards on federally financed construction projects and in connection with other large federal contracts. Executive Order 11246, as presently administered by the Office of Federal Contract Compliance Programs, requires that all employers with 50 or more employees and federal contracts in excess of $50,000 file written affirmative action plans with the government. These must include minority and female hiring goals and timetables to which the contractor must commit its "good faith" efforts. Race and gender considerations—which may include numerical goals—are also a fundamental aspect of affirmative action planning by federal departments and agencies to eliminate minority and female "underrepresentation" at various levels of agency employment.[6]

Federal contract "set-asides" and minority subcontracting goals evolved from Small Business Administration programs to foster participation in the federal procurement process by small disadvantaged businesses (SDBs), or small businesses owned and controlled by "socially and economically disadvantaged" individuals.[7] Minority group members and women are presumed to be socially and economically disadvantaged under the Small Business Act, while non-minority contractors must present evidence to prove their eligibility. "Goals" or "set-asides" for minority groups, women, and other "disadvantaged" individuals have also been routinely included in federal funding measures for education, defense, transportation, and other activities over much of the last two decades. Currently, each federal department and agency must contribute to achieving a government-wide, annual procurement goal of at least 5% with its own goal-oriented effort to create "maximum practicable opportunity" for minority and female contractors.[8] In addition, 10% of federal highway and surface transportation project funds must be set aside for small disadvantaged firms through the end of FY2009.[9]

By the mid-1980s, the Supreme Court had approved the temporary remedial use of race- or gender-conscious selection criteria by private employers under Title VII. These measures were deemed a proper remedy for "manifest racial imbalance" in "traditionally segregated" job categories, if voluntarily adopted by the employer,[10] or for entrenched patterns of "egregious and longstanding" discrimination by the employer, if imposed by judicial decree.[11] In either circumstance, however, the Court required proof of remedial justification rooted in the employer's own past discrimination and its persistent workplace effects. Thus, a "firm basis" in evidence, as revealed by a "manifest imbalance"—or "historic," "persistent," and "egregious" underrepresentation—of minorities or women in affected job categories was deemed an essential predicate to preferential affirmative action. Of equal importance, all racial preferences in employment were to be judged in terms of their adverse impact on "identifiable" non-minority group members. Remedies that protected minorities from layoff, for example, were most suspect and unlikely to pass muster if they displaced more senior white workers.[12] But the consideration of race or gender as a "plus" factor in employment decisions, when it did not unduly hinder or "trammel" the "legitimate expectations" of non-minority employees, won ready judicial acceptance. Affirmative action preferences, however, had to be sufficiently flexible, temporary in duration, and "narrowly tailored" to avoid becoming rigid "quotas."[13]

The *Regents of the University of California v. Bakke* ruling in 1978 launched the contemporary constitutional debate over state-sponsored affirmative action. A "notable lack of unanimity" was evident from the six separate opinions filed in that case. One four-Justice plurality in *Bakke* voted to strike down as a violation of Title VI a special admissions program of the University of California at Davis medical school which set aside sixteen of one hundred positions in each incoming class for minority students, where the institution itself was not shown to have discriminated in the past. Another bloc of four Justices argued that racial classifications designed to further remedial purposes were foreclosed neither by the Constitution nor the Civil Rights Act and would have upheld the minority admissions quota. Justice Powell added a fifth vote to each camp by condemning the Davis program on equal protection grounds while endorsing the nonexclusive consideration of race as an admissions criteria to foster student diversity.[14]

In Justice Powell's view, neither the state's asserted interest in remedying "societal discrimination," nor of providing "role models" for minority students was sufficiently "compelling" to warrant the use of a "suspect" racial classification in the admission process. But the attainment of a "diverse student body" was, for Justice Powell, "clearly a permissible goal for an institution of higher education" since diversity of minority viewpoints furthered "academic freedom," a "special concern of the First Amendment."[15] Accordingly, race could be considered by a university as a "plus" or "one element of a range of factors"—even if it "tipped the scale" among qualified applicants—as long as it "did not insulate the individual from comparison with all the other candidates for the available seats."[16] The "quota" in *Bakke* was infirm, however, since it defined diversity only in racial terms and absolutely excluded non-minorities from a given number of seats. By two 5-to-4 votes, therefore, the Supreme Court affirmed the lower court order admitting Bakke but reversed the judicial ban on consideration of race in admissions.

The Powell opinion in *Bakke* may help to explain the conflicting results reached by the Court in the Michigan Law School and undergraduate admissions cases. In *Grutter v. Bollinger*,[17] a 5 to 4 majority of the Justices, led by Justice O'Connor, held that the University's Law School had a "compelling" interest in the "educational benefits that flow from a diverse student body," which justified its consideration of race in admissions to assemble a "critical mass" of "underrepresented" minority students. But in *Gratz v. Bollinger*,[18] six Justices decided that the University's undergraduate policy of awarding "racial bonus points" to minority applicants was not "narrowly tailored" enough to pass constitutional muster. The law school program was deemed constitutional because it was based on an individualized, holistic review of each applicant's file, in contrast to the undergraduate program, which "[did] not provide for a meaningful individualized review of applicants" but instead "assign[ed] every underrepresented minority applicant the same, automatic 20-point bonus without consideration of the particular background, experiences, or qualities of each individual applicant."[19] In effect, *Grutter* enshrined in law the Powell diversity rationale—embraced by no other Justice in *Bakke*—that the state has a "compelling" interest in promoting racial diversity in higher education.

More recently, the Court agreed to review new legal questions regarding racial diversity in education. Although the *Grutter* and *Gratz* decisions settled the question of whether race-based policies to promote diversity in higher education are ever constitutionally acceptable, the cases did not address whether diversity is a permissible goal in the elementary and secondary educational setting. To resolve this question, the Supreme Court agreed to review two cases that involved the use of race to maintain racially diverse public schools in Seattle and Louisville. In *Parents Involved in Community Schools v. Seattle School District No. 1*, a consolidated ruling that resolved both cases, the Court, in a fractured decision, struck down the school plans at issue, holding that they violated the equal protection guarantee of the Fourteenth Amendment.[20] Announcing the judgment of the Court was Chief Justice Roberts, who led a plurality of four Justices in concluding that the school plans were unconstitutional because they did not serve a compelling governmental interest. Although Justice Kennedy concurred in the Court's judgment striking down the plans, he declined to sign on to the plurality opinion in full, in part because he disagreed with its implication that diversity in elementary and secondary education, at least as properly defined, does not serve a compelling governmental interest. According to Justice Kennedy, "[d]iversity, depending on its meaning and definition, is a compelling educational goal a school district may pursue,"[21] but neither Seattle nor Louisville had shown that its plans served a compelling interest in promoting diversity or that the plans were narrowly tailored to achieve that goal. The Court's ruling appears to indicate that race-conscious measures to promote racial diversity in public education remain constitutionally permissible in theory, although in practice it is less clear what types of programs the Court would consider to be sufficiently narrowly tailored to pass constitutional muster.[22]

In another series of decisions, the Court approved of congressionally mandated racial preferences to allocate the benefits of contracts on federally sponsored public works projects, *Fullilove v. Klutznick*,[23] while condemning similar actions taken by local governmental entities to promote public contracting opportunities for minority entrepreneurs, *City of Richmond v. J.A. Croson Co.*[24] Contextual differences in the particular kind of governmental activity being challenged frequently account for variations in judicial approach to affirmative action in public employment, government contracting, admission to public institutions of higher education, and election redistricting.[25] Almost uniformly, however, the law has been marked by a failure of consensus on most issues, with bare majorities, pluralities, or—as in *Bakke*—a single Justice, determining the "law" of the case.

Not until 1989 did a majority of the Justices resolve the proper constitutional standard for review of governmental classifications by race enacted for a remedial or other "benign" legislative purpose. Disputes prior to the *City of Richmond* case yielded divergent views as to whether state affirmative action measures for the benefit of racial minorities were subject to the same "strict scrutiny" as applied to "invidious" racial discrimination under the Equal Protection Clause, an "intermediate" standard resembling the test for gender-based classifications, or simple rationality. In *City of Richmond,* a 5 to 4 majority settled on strict scrutiny to invalidate a 30% set-aside of city contracts for minority-owned businesses because the program was not "narrowly tailored" to a "compelling" governmental interest. While "race-conscious" remedies could be legislated in response to proven past discrimination by the affected governmental entities, "racial balancing" untailored to "specific" and "identified" evidence of minority exclusion was impermissible. *City of Richmond* suggested, however, that because of its unique equal protection enforcement authority, a constitutional standard more tolerant of racial line-drawing may apply to Congress. This conclusion was reinforced a year later when, in *Metro Broadcasting, Inc. v. FCC*,[26] the Court upheld certain preferences for minorities in broadcast licensing proceedings, approved by Congress not as a remedy for past discrimination but to promote the "important" governmental interest in "broadcast diversity."

This two-tiered approach to equal protection analysis of governmental affirmative action was short-lived, however. In *Adarand Constructors, Inc. v. Pena,*[27] the Court applied "strict scrutiny" to a federal transportation program of financial incentives for prime contractors who subcontracted to firms owned by "socially and economically disadvantaged individuals," defined so as to prefer members of designated racial minorities. Although the Court refrained from deciding the constitutional merits of the particular program before it, and remanded for further proceedings below, it determined that all "racial classifications" by government at any level must be justified by a "compelling governmental interest" and "narrowly tailored" to that end. But the majority opinion, by Justice O'Connor, sought to "dispel the notion" that "strict scrutiny is 'strict in theory, but fatal in fact,'" by acknowledging a role for Congress as architect of remedies for discrimination nationwide. "The unhappy persistence of both the practices and lingering effects of racial discrimination against minorities in this country is an unfortunate reality, and the government is not disqualified from acting in response to it." No further guidance is provided, however, as to the scope of remedial power remaining in congressional hands, or of the conditions required for its exercise. Bottom line, *Adarand* suggests that racial preferences in federal law are a remedy of last resort, which must be adequately justified and narrowly drawn to pass constitutional muster. In the post-*Adarand* era, lower federal courts have at times upheld and at other times struck down government programs that contain minority contracting preferences. For example, in a recent and highly significant minority contracting case, the Federal Circuit held that the Department of Defense's (DOD's) Small Disadvantaged Business (SDB) program was unconstitutional.[28]

## End Notes

[1] See, e.g., Green v. County Bd., 391 U.S. 430 (1968); Swann v. Bd. of Educ., 402 U.S. 1 (1971); Keyes v. Denver Sch. Dist., 413 U.S. 189 (1973).

[2] Dowell v. Bd. of Educ., 498 U.S. 237 (1991). See also Freeman v. Pitts, 503 U.S. 467 (1993); Missouri v. Jenkins, 515 U.S. 70 (1995).

[3] 42 U.S.C. §§ 2000e et seq.

[4] Id. at 2000d et seq.

[5] 34 C.F.R. § 100.3(b)(vii)(6).

[6] 42 U.S.C. § 2000e-16(b)(1); 5 U.S.C. § 7201. The Equal Employment Opportunity Commission and the Office of Personnel Management have issued rules to guide implementation and monitoring of minority recruitment programs by individual federal agencies. Among various other specified requirements, each agency plan "must include specific determinations of underrepresentation for each group and must be accompanied by quantifiable indices by which progress toward eliminating underrepresentation can be measured." 5 C.F.R. § 720.205(b).

[7] 15 U.S.C.§ 637 (a), (d).

[8] 15 U.S.C. § 644(g)(1).

[9] § 1101 of P.L. 109-59, the "Safe, Accountable, Flexible, and Efficient Transportation Equity Act of 2005" carried forward prior longstanding USDOT policy mandating a 10 percent SDB set-side "[e]xcept to the extent the Secretary of Transportation determines" otherwise.

[10] United Steelworkers v. Weber, 443 U.S. 193 (1979).

[11] Local 28 Sheet Metal Workers v. EEOC, 478 U.S. 421 (1986).

[12] Wygant v. Jackson Bd. of Educ., 476 U.S. 267 (1986).

[13] United States v. Paradise, 480 U.S. 149 (1987); Johnson v. Transp. Agency, 480 U.S. 616 (1987). For additional information, see CRS Report RL30470, *Affirmative Action in Employment: A Legal Overview*, by Jody Feder.

[14] Regents of the Univ. of California v. Bakke, 438 U.S. 265 (1975).

[15] Id. at 311-12.

[16] Id. at 317.

[17] 539 U.S. 506 (2003).

[18] 539 U.S. 244 (2003).

[19] Id. at 276-77 (O'Connor. J., concurring).

[20] 127 S. Ct. 2738 (2007).

[21] Id. at 2789.

[22] For more information, see CRS Report RL30410, *Affirmative Action and Diversity in Public Education: Legal Developments*, by Jody Feder.

[23] 448 U.S. 448 (1980).

[24] 488 U.S. 469 (1989).

[25] See, e.g., League of United Latin Am. Citizens v. Perry, 548 U.S. 399 (2006); Shaw v. Reno, 509 U.S. 630 (1993).

[26] 497 U.S. 547 (1990).

[27] 515 U.S. 200 (1995). For more information on *Adarand* and minority contracting, see CRS Report RL33284, *Minority Contracting and Affirmative Action for Disadvantaged Small Businesses: Legal Issues*, by Jody Feder.

[28] Rothe Dev. Corp. v. DOD, 545 F.3d 1023 (Fed. Cir. 2008).

In: Affirmative Action and Preferential Treatment ISBN: 978-1-62257-465-0
Editors: P. L. Medina and J. E. Patel 

*Chapter 3*

# AFFIRMATIVE ACTION IN EMPLOYMENT: A LEGAL OVERVIEW*

***Jody Feder***

## SUMMARY

This report discusses current constitutional and statutory requirements related to affirmative action in employment. Seeds of the legal controversy regarding affirmative action may be traced to the early 1960s as the Supreme Court grappled with the seemingly intractable problem of racial segregation in the nation's public schools. Judicial rulings from this period recognized an "affirmative duty," cast upon local school boards by the Equal Protection Clause of the U.S. Constitution, to desegregate formerly "dual school" systems and to eliminate "root and branch" the last "vestiges" of state-enforced segregation. In the employment context, the Court has similarly upheld the constitutionality of affirmative action plans adopted by or imposed upon governmental entities with a history of past discrimination. Meanwhile, Congress and the Executive have followed the Court's lead by approving a panoply of laws and regulations that authorize, either directly or by judicial or administrative interpretation, "race-conscious" strategies to promote minority opportunity in jobs, education, and governmental contracting.

The basic statutory framework for affirmative action in employment derives from Title VII of the Civil Rights Act of 1964, which prohibits

---

* This is an edited, reformatted and augmented version of Congressional Research Service, Publication No. RL30470, dated January 19, 2010.

employment discrimination on the basis of race, color, national origin, religion, and sex. The Title VII remedial scheme rests largely on judicial power to order monetary damages and injunctive relief, including "such affirmative action as may be appropriate," to make discrimination victims whole. Except as may be imposed by order of a court to remedy "egregious" violations of law, however, or by consent decree to settle pending claims, there is no general statutory obligation on employers to adopt affirmative action plans. However, the Equal Employment Opportunity Commission (EEOC) has issued guidelines to protect employers and unions from charges of "reverse discrimination" when they voluntarily take actions to eliminate the effects of past discrimination. In addition, federal departments and agencies are required to periodically formulate affirmative action plans for their employees and a "minority recruitment program" to correct minority "underrepresentation" in specific federal job categories.

The historical model for federal laws and regulations establishing minority participation "goals" may be found in Executive Orders which since the early 1960s have imposed affirmative minority hiring and employment requirements on federally financed construction projects and in connection with other large federal contracts. Executive Order 11246, as presently administered by the Office of Federal Contract Compliance Programs, requires that all employers with 50 or more employees and federal contracts in excess of $50,000 file written affirmative action plans with the government. These must include minority and female hiring goals and timetables to which the contractor must commit its "good faith" efforts.

## INTRODUCTION

This report discusses current constitutional and statutory requirements related to affirmative action in employment. Seeds of the legal controversy regarding affirmative action may be traced to the early 1960s as first the Warren and then the Burger Court grappled with the seemingly intractable problem of racial segregation in the nation's public schools. Judicial rulings from this period recognized an "affirmative duty," cast upon local school boards by the Equal Protection Clause, to desegregate formerly "dual school" systems and to eliminate "root and branch" the last "vestiges" of state-enforced segregation.[1] In the employment context, the Court has similarly upheld the constitutionality of affirmative action plans adopted by or imposed upon governmental entities with a history of past discrimination. Meanwhile, Congress and the Executive followed the Court's lead by approving a panoply of laws and regulations which authorize, either directly or by judicial or administrative interpretation, "race-conscious" strategies to promote minority opportunity in jobs, education, and governmental contracting.

The basic statutory framework for affirmative action in employment derives from Title VII of the Civil Rights Act of 1964, which prohibits employment discrimination on the basis of race, color, national origin, religion, or sex.[2] The Title VII remedial scheme rests largely on judicial power to order monetary damages and injunctive relief, including "such affirmative action as may be appropriate,"[3] to make discrimination victims whole. Except as may be imposed by order of a court to remedy "egregious" violations of law, however, or by consent decree to settle pending claims, there is no general statutory obligation on employers to adopt affirmative action plans. However, the Equal Employment Opportunity Commission (EEOC) has issued guidelines to protect employers and unions from charges of "reverse discrimination" when they voluntarily take actions to eliminate the effects of past discrimination. In addition, federal departments and agencies are required to periodically formulate affirmative action plans for their employees and a "minority recruitment program" to correct minority "underrepresentation" in specific federal job categories.[4]

The historical model for federal laws and regulations establishing minority participation "goals" may be found in Executive Orders which since the early 1960s have imposed affirmative minority hiring and employment requirements on federally financed construction projects and in connection with other large federal contracts. Executive Order 11246, as currently administered by the Office of Federal Contract Compliance Programs, requires that all employers with 50 or more employees and federal contracts in excess of $50,000 file written affirmative action plans with the government. These must include minority and female hiring goals and timetables to which the contractor must commit its "good faith" efforts. Smaller contractors are bound by the nondiscrimination requirements of the Executive Order, but are not required to maintain formal written programs.[5] Judicial decisions early on upheld the executive order program as a constitutionally valid governmental response to racial segregation in the construction trades and affected industries.

By the mid-1980s, the Supreme Court had approved the temporary remedial use of race- or gender-conscious selection criteria by private employers under Title VII. These measures were deemed a proper remedy for "manifest racial imbalance" in "traditionally segregated" job categories, if voluntarily adopted by the employer,[6] or for entrenched patterns of "egregious and longstanding" discrimination by the employer, if imposed by judicial decree.[7] In either circumstance, however, the Court required proof of remedial justification rooted in the employer's own past discrimination and its persistent workplace effects. Thus, a "firm basis" in evidence, as revealed by a "manifest imbalance"—or "historic," "persistent," and "egregious" underrepresentation — of minorities or women in affected job categories was deemed an essential predicate to preferential affirmative action. Of equal importance, all racial preferences in employment were to be judged in terms of their adverse impact on "identifiable" non-minority group members. But the consideration of race or gender as a "plus" factor in employment decisions, when it did not unduly hinder or "trammel" the "legitimate expectations" of non-minority employees, won ready judicial acceptance.[8] Affirmative action preferences, however, had to be sufficiently flexible, temporary in duration, and "narrowly tailored" to avoid becoming rigid "quotas."

Judicial precedents on affirmative action in employment have developed along two concurrent but not necessarily coterminous lines. One line of authority delineates the permissible scope of affirmative action imposed by judicial decree to remedy proven violations of Title VII or the Constitution. The other involves the validity of voluntary affirmative action plans by public and private employers. Several basic principles emerge from the case law.

First, a fundamental prerequisite to the adoption of minority goals or preferences is a remedial justification rooted in the employer's own past discrimination and its persistent workplace effects. Stricter probative standards mandated by the Constitution may bind public employers in this regard than apply to private employers under Title VII. Basically, a "firm basis" in evidence—as revealed by a "manifest imbalance," or "persistent" and "egregious" disparities in the employment of minorities or women in affected job categories—has been viewed by the courts as an essential predicate for affirmative action preferences.

Secondly, beyond a record of past discrimination by the employer, all affirmative action plans are judged in terms of the burden they place on identifiable non-minorities. Thus, remedies that immediately result in the displacement of more senior white male employees—like promotion preferences or minority group protections against layoff—are most suspect and least likely to pass legal or constitutional muster. At the other end of the spectrum, hiring or recruitment goals or preferences that do not "unnecessarily trammel" the "legitimate expectations" for advancement of non-minority candidates are more likely to win judicial acceptance. Finally, all "race-conscious" affirmative action remedies must be sufficiently flexible, temporary in duration, and "narrowly tailored" so as to avoid becoming rigid "quotas."

## JUDICIAL AFFIRMATIVE ACTION REMEDIES

Even before the Supreme Court had spoken, every federal circuit court of appeals, in cases dating back to the very inception of the 1964 Civil Rights Act, had approved use of race or gender preferences to remedy "historic," "egregious," or "longstanding" discrimination. This line of judicial authority was ratified by the Court's rulings in *Local 28, Sheetmetal Workers v. EEOC* and *United States v. Paradise.*[9] The former involved contempt proceedings against a union with an established history of racial and ethnic discrimination for its willful violation of a judicially imposed 29% minority membership goal. To remedy years of union evasion, amounting to contempt of court, the Second Circuit had approved an order reinstating the minority membership goal and requiring that job referrals be made on the basis of one apprentice for every four journeyman. The Supreme Court affirmed, five to four.

In the opinion, a plurality of four Justices held that Title VII does not preclude race-conscious affirmative action as a "last resort" for cases of "persistent or egregious" discrimination, or to dissipate the "lingering effects of pervasive discrimination," but that, in most cases, only "make whole" relief—in the form of back pay or specific hiring orders—for individual victims is required. The plurality also felt that by twice adjusting the union's deadline, and because of the district court's "otherwise flexible application of the membership goal," the remedy had been enforced as a "benchmark" of the union's compliance "rather than as a strict racial quota." Rounding out the five-Justice majority was Justice Powell, who emphasized the history of "contemptuous racial discrimination" revealed by the record, and the temporary and flexible nature of the remedy. Meanwhile, one group of dissenting Justices found the referral quota excessive because economic conditions in the construction industry made compliance impracticable, while the other dissenters read Title VII to bar all judicially-ordered race-conscious relief for the benefit of non-victims.

A parallel situation was presented by *Paradise*. In 1972, to remedy nearly four decades of systematic exclusion of blacks from the ranks of the Alabama State troopers, the district court ordered a hiring quota and enjoined the state from discriminating in regard to promotions. Seven years later, a series of consent decrees calling for new nondiscriminatory promotion procedures was approved to rectify the total dearth of black troopers in the upper ranks. In the interim, however, the court ordered a one-to-one racial quota for the rank of corporal and above, provided sufficient qualified blacks were available, until 25% of each rank was black. Only one round of promotions for corporal was made before the quota for that and the sergeant rank was suspended. The Supreme Court granted review of the order under the Equal Protection Clause.

A plurality of four Justices considered several factors in determining whether the plan violated the equal protection rights of white troopers: the necessity of the relief and the efficacy of alternative remedies, the plan's flexibility and duration, the relationship between the plan's numerical goals and the relevant labor market, and the plan's impact on the rights of third parties. Significant was the fact that the order did not require the promotion of anyone and could be waived in the absence of qualified minority candidates, as it already had been with respect to lieutenant and captain positions. It was also tied to the percentage of minorities in the area workforce, 25%. Finally, because it did not bar white advancement, but merely postponed it, the plan did not impose unacceptable burdens on innocent third parties.

The plurality opinion therefore concluded that the promotion quota was "narrowly tailored" and justified by the government's "compelling" interest in eradicating the state's "pervasive, systematic, and obstinate exclusion" of blacks and its history of resistance to the court's orders. Justice Stevens, who provided the fifth vote for the Court's judgment, stated in a separate opinion that the district court did not exceed the bounds of "reasonableness" in devising a remedy. One group of dissenting Justices, however, found the plan "cannot survive judicial scrutiny" because the one-to-one promotion quota is not sufficiently tied to the percentage of blacks eligible for promotion, while a separate dissenting opinion stated simply that the district court "exceeded its equitable powers."

## VOLUNTARY AFFIRMATIVE ACTION

The remedial justification for voluntary affirmative action in employment was explored by the Court in *Wygant v. Jackson Board of Education.*[10] A collective bargaining agreement between the school board and the teacher's union in that case provided a hiring preference for minority teachers coupled with layoff protection until the minority composition of the faculty mirrored that of the student body district wide. Seniority was to govern layoffs except that in no event were overall minority faculty percentages to be reduced. In the face of a constitutional challenge by ten laid-off white teachers, the Court voided the minority layoff provision, but no particular rationale commanded majority support.

Seven members of the *Wygant* Court agreed that some forms of voluntary affirmative action may be constitutionally justifiable on the part of a governmental entity itself guilty of past discrimination. However, neither the asserted interest in the presence of minority teachers as critical "role models," or to ameliorate "societal discrimination," provided "compelling" justification for the layoff plan absent "convincing" evidence of the board's own past discrimination. Moreover, while innocent non-minorities could be made to share some of the burden, the remedy could not intrude too severely upon their rights. Because the minority layoff protection in *Wygant* "impose[d] the entire burden of achieving racial equality on particular individuals," Justice Powell concluded that innocent third parties were impacted too heavily. In this respect, the layoff provision was distinguishable from preferential hiring decisions, which "diffuse" the burden more generally. Reserving judgment on the hiring issue, Justice White concurred that the layoff remedy went too far because it displaced more senior white employees in favor of minorities who were not actual discrimination victims. In a separate concurrence, Justice O'Connor aligned herself with the Powell view that societal discrimination will not justify voluntary affirmative action remedies, and that the layoff plan was infirm because it was overbroad and not "narrowly tailored" to the board's past discrimination.

Significantly, *Wygant* was a constitutional case decided on Fourteenth Amendment equal protection principles. Corollary issues concerning voluntary affirmative action plans adopted by private employers under Title VII reached the Court in *United Steelworkers v. Weber*.[11] The *Weber* case upheld a voluntary affirmative action plan by a private employer, including a minority quota for a craft training program, to rectify "manifest racial imbalance in traditionally segregated job categories." The Court required no specific finding of past discrimination by the employer, deciding the case instead on the basis of the historically well established record of nationwide bias in trade union membership.

In 1974, the employer and union in *Weber* negotiated an affirmative action plan to increase the percentage of blacks in skilled craft positions from 2% to the level of their overall participation in the area workforce, or 39%. By reserving half of the company's craft training program slots for minorities, several white employees were passed over in favor of less senior blacks. There was no evidence that the under-representation of minorities in craft jobs was attributable to past discrimination by the employer. Nonetheless, relying on general judicial and research findings relative to nationwide patterns of minority exclusion from trade union membership, the Supreme Court ruled five to two that "racial preferences" in the program were a lawful means to combat "manifest racial imbalance" in craft positions resulting from "old patterns of racial segregation and hierarchy."

Conceding that Title VII could literally be read to bar all race-conscious employment practices, the Court decided that the purpose of the act, rather than its literal meaning, controlled. The legislative history and context from which the act arose, Justice Brennan wrote, compelled the conclusion that the primary purpose of Title VII was to "open employment opportunities for Negroes in occupations which have traditionally been closed to them." Accordingly, "[i]t would be ironic indeed" to read the statute to preclude "all voluntary, private, race-conscious efforts" to abolish workplace segregation. Moreover, the specific plan in question, mandating a one to one racial ratio until a specific minority participation rate is achieved, was permissible affirmative action because it did "not unnecessarily trammel the interest of white employees."[12] *Weber* thus permitted private employers to implement certain forms of temporary affirmative action to advance minority employment opportunities, even where such measures have an incidental adverse impact on white workers.

In *Johnson v. Transportation Agency,*[13] the Court reviewed a voluntary affirmative action plan adopted by a public employer, the Transportation Agency of Santa Clara County, California. That plan authorized the agency to consider the gender of applicants as one factor for promotion to positions within traditionally segregated job classifications in which women had been underrepresented. Women were significantly underrepresented in the county's labor force as a whole and in five of seven job categories, including skilled crafts where all 238 employees were men. The plan's long range goal was proportional representation. However, because of the small number of positions and low turnover, actual implementation was based on short term goals which were adjusted annually and took account of qualified minority and female availability. No specific numerical goals or quotas were used.

The petitioner in *Johnson* was a male employee who had applied for promotion to the position of road dispatcher, only to be rejected in favor of a female competitor. Both the petitioner and the woman who won the promotion were deemed well qualified for the position, although the petitioner had scored slightly higher in the first round interview. The appointing official for the agency indicated that in reaching the decision to promote the female candidate, he had considered the candidates' qualifications, backgrounds, test scores, and expertise as well as gender considerations.

The Supreme Court upheld the county's action, six to three. Justice Brennan decided for the majority that Title VII was not coextensive with the Constitution and that, therefore, *Weber* not *Wygant* was controlling. The noted disparities in female workforce participation satisfied the *Weber* requirement for a "manifest imbalance" since to require any additional showing could expose the employer to discrimination lawsuits and operate as a disincentive to voluntary compliance with the statute. The Court likened the county plan to the treatment of race as a "plus" factor in the "Harvard Plan" for higher educational admissions approved by Justice Powell in the *Bakke* case.[14] Because sex was but one factor in the decision-making process, no applicant was excluded from participation on account of sex. In a caveat, however, the Court warned that "[i]f a plan failed to take distinction in qualification into account in providing for actual employment decision, it would dictate mere blind hiring by the numbers," and would be invalid because "it would hold supervisors to achievement of a particular percentage of minority employment or membership ... regardless of circumstances such as economic conditions or the number of available qualified minority applicants ... "[15]

Justice White, dissenting, would have overruled *Weber* as a "perversion" of Title VII, as would Justices Scalia and the Chief Justice, joining in a separate dissent. The dissenters criticized the majority for using Title VII "to overcome the effect not of the employer's own discrimination, but of societal attitudes that have limited entry of certain races, or of a particular sex, into certain jobs." Noting the district court finding of no past discrimination by the county agency, they argued in light of *Sheetmetal Workers* that "there is no sensible basis for construing Title VII to permit employers to engage in race- or sex-conscious employment practices that courts would be forbidden from ordering them to engage in following a judicial finding of discrimination."

To date, therefore, the Supreme Court has permitted race-conscious hiring criteria by private employers under Title VII, either as a remedy for past discrimination or to redress a "conspicuous racial imbalance in traditionally segregated job categories," but refused to find that a state's interest in faculty diversity to provide teacher "role models" was sufficiently compelling to warrant a race-conscious layoff policy. Lower courts are similarly divided, though a few have applied an "operational need analysis" to uphold police force diversity policies, recognizing "that 'a law enforcement body's need to carry out its mission effectively, with a workforce that appears unbiased, is able to communicate with the public and is respected by the community it serves,' may constitute a compelling state interest."[16]

A three-judge panel of the Seventh Circuit has pressed the legal debate one step further by relying on the student diversity rulings in the Michigan cases[17] to uphold Chicago Police Department's affirmative action hiring program. The decision in *Petit v. City of Chicago*[18] found that large urban police departments have an "even more compelling need for diversity" than universities and affirmed the Chicago police program "under the *Grutter* standards." A "strong basis" for affirmative action was provided by expert testimony that the city's minority residents deeply distrusted police, and that creating a diverse force at the sergeant rank would "set a proper tone" in the department to earn the trust of the community. Outside of law enforcement, however, courts generally allow for consideration of race in hiring and promotion decisions only in response to demonstrable evidence of past discrimination by the employer or within the affected industry. No rule of deference like that extended to educational institutions has been recognized for employers, nor is one necessarily implied by the Michigan cases.

In recent years, voluntary affirmative action measures appear to have become somewhat disfavored in the employment context, although related issues continue to be litigated. For example, in 2009 the Supreme Court issued a decision in *Ricci v. DeStafano*,[19] a Title VII case questioning whether the New Haven Fire Department could set aside the results of a promotion exam that would have disproportionately made more white firefighters eligible for promotion than minority firefighters. After the city set aside the test results, the white firefighters sued, claiming reverse discrimination, but the city argued that its actions were necessary in order to avoid subsequent charges of racial bias for implementing a test with a discriminatory effect. Ultimately, the Court ruled in favor of the white firefighters, holding that the city had violated Title VII's prohibition against disparate treatment when it discarded the test results. Although the case did not involve affirmative action, the decision may make it more difficult for employers to voluntarily comply with Title VII by implementing affirmative action plans or by altering employment policies or practices that have an unintentionally discriminatory effect.[20]

## AFFIRMATIVE ACTION CONSENT DECREES

State and local programs mandating affirmative action in employment initially met with greater judicial approval than public contracting preferences for minorities in the wake of the Supreme Court's decision in *City of Richmond v. J.A. Croson and Co.*[21] This may be due, in part, to the fact that employment preferences are frequently, though not always, linked to settlements of individual or class action lawsuits. Depending on the stage of proceedings, a formal record of past discrimination may already have developed when agreement is reached. At the very least, there is usually some allegation of misconduct by the public employer. In addition, there may be underlying judicial findings of discrimination or district court involvement in fashioning or approving the consent decree, both of which are factors traditionally prompting deference by appellate courts when reviewing affirmative action efforts.[22]

Between 1972 and 1983, the Department of Justice sued 106 public employers; of those, 93 were settled by consent decree. These court-approved agreements typically set goals and timetables for increasing minority and female under-representation in the workforce. Of the cases that the Justice Department still monitors, many stem from litigation dating back to the 1970s, mainly against police and fire departments.[23] Under *Croson* and, subsequently, *Adarand Constructors, Inc. v. Pena,*[24] however, these orders and consent decrees have come under "strict scrutiny." For example, a major ruling by the Eleventh Circuit in 1994 invalidated a consent decree involving the Birmingham, Alabama fire department for being an "entirely arbitrary" fixed quota that unduly restricted opportunities for whites,[25] and judicial rulings in Boston forced abandonment of a 1980 consent decree, which established a race-based policy for promoting sergeants.[26] Indeed, a number of cities and states have successfully fought consent decrees and ended federal monitoring of their minority hiring practices.

In 1999, the Supreme Court declined to review a Fifth Circuit decision striking down the Dallas Fire Department's affirmative action plan. In *City of Dallas v. Dallas Fire Fighters Association,*[27] the appellate panel held that there was insufficient evidence of past discrimination in the Dallas Fire Department to justify the department's policy of promoting some women and minorities over white males who had achieved scores within the same "band" on a civil service examination. Evidence of discrimination in the record consisted of a 1976 consent decree between the city and the Justice Department finding impermissible racial discrimination by the city under Title VII, and statistical underrepresentation of minorities in the ranks to which the challenged promotions were made. The court recognized that "out-of-rank promotions do not impose as great a burden on non-minorities as would layoff or discharge." But it found that interference by the city with "legitimate expectations" of promotion based on exam performance was unjustified where alternative remedies were not yet exhausted, and there was no proof of "a history of egregious and pervasive discrimination or resistance to affirmative action that has warranted more serious measures in other cases."[28] Even less evidence of past sex discrimination was found by the court to justify the city's gender-based discrimination.

In *Ensley Branch, NAACP v. Seibels,*[29] the Eleventh Circuit rejected both long term and annual goals imposed by consent decree for the hiring of firefighters and police officers by the City of Birmingham, Alabama. The main fault with the city's affirmative action plan was that it had become a permanent alternative to the development of nondiscriminatory tests and other valid selection procedures. Rather than ending discrimination, the long-term goals in the plan were "designed to create parity between the racial composition of the labor pool and the race of the employees in each job position." Annual hiring goals had been arbitrarily set at twenty-five to fifty percent for minorities and had been "mechanically" applied as "rigid quotas," in the court's view, without regard to "relative qualifications" of the candidates. On remand, the district court was ordered to "re-write the decrees to relate the annual goals to the proportion of blacks in the relevant, objectively qualified labor pool" and "to make clear that the annual goals cannot last indefinitely."[30]

Likewise, an affirmative action promotional plan for the Maryland State Police, agreed to by the parties with consent of a federal district court, was subjected to strict scrutiny review and found wanting by the Fourth Circuit in *Maryland Troopers Ass'n v. Evans.*[31] Specifically, goals linked to minority representation in the general population, instead of the qualified labor pool, were found deficient under *Croson* analysis, as was the failure to first exhaust all race-neutral alternative means of increasing minority opportunity. The latter factor has frequently been determinative of the constitutional question in the judicial mind.[32] *Croson* was also applied by the Sixth Circuit to defeat a 50% minority goal for the rank of sergeant in the Detroit Police Department, which had been in effect for nearly two decades, since "limiting the duration of a race-conscious remedy which clearly impacts adversely on [nonminorities] is a keystone of a narrowly tailored plan."[33] Failure to satisfy the court as to the cause of apparent statistical disparities with respect to minority employment,[34] the scope or duration of the remedy,[35] the absence of a provision for waiver where qualified minority candidates were unavailable,[36] and the consequent undue burden placed on nonminorities[37] are all factors that have led to judicial invalidation of state and local affirmative action.

## AFFIRMATIVE RECRUITMENT AND OUTREACH PROGRAMS

The Court arguably has yet to precisely define "racial classification" for equal protection purposes, but a plurality of Justices have described the concept in terms of burdens or benefits placed on individuals because of race, or subjecting individuals to unequal treatment. Race-conscious action by government or private employers that neither confers a benefit nor imposes a burden on individuals may not be subject to strict scrutiny or heightened judicial review. Thus, courts have not found data collection activities concerning the racial or gender makeup of a workforce to violate the Constitution. "Statistical information as such is a rather neutral entity which only becomes meaningful when it is interpreted."[38] Similarly, strict scrutiny has generally not been applied by the courts to minority outreach or recruitment efforts that do not amount to an actual preference in employment decisionmaking. A public university, for example, may be racially "aware" or "conscious" by amassing statistics on the racial and ethnic makeup of its faculty and encouraging broader recruiting of racial or ethnic minorities, without triggering strict scrutiny equal protection review. These activities do not impose burdens or benefits, it has been held, nor do they subject individuals to unequal treatment. If that institution, however, then engages in race-preferential hiring, firing, or promotion, that action is subject to strict scrutiny. This distinction between "inclusive" forms of affirmative action—such as recruitment, advertising in minority media, and other outreach to minority communities—and "exclusive" affirmative action—such as quotas, set-asides, or layoff preferences—has featured prominently in many decisions.[39]

One of the first post-*Adarand* decisions, *Shuford v. State Board of Education*,[40] upheld provisions similar to E.O. 11246 in the face of constitutional challenge. A consent decree between the State Board of Education and separate classes of white and black women had addressed issues of hiring and promotion within the Alabama system. In addition to a standard nondiscrimination clause, the decree required yearly reports tracking the number of new women hires, procedures for expanding the pool of female applicants, numerical hiring goals, and parity for women in the personnel selection process. Specifically prohibited by the decree, however, were set-asides, quotas, and the selection of less qualified candidates based on race or gender.

Because expanding the pool of qualified minority or female candidates by "inclusive" recruitment and outreach only added to the competition faced by non-class members—in this case, white males—and did not result in lost job opportunities and promotions, the court avoided the traditional Title VII and equal protection analysis applied to "exclusive" affirmative action techniques. It upheld the annual statistical report requirement of the decree since "the attempt to ascertain whether there is a problem and whether progress is being made should be encouraged."[41] Affirmative recruitment of qualified female candidates was similarly acceptable so long as the recruitment did not exclude male applicants. Thus, "if the postsecondary system began recruiting at black and women's colleges and stopped recruiting at Auburn, this would be an instance of exclusion."[42]

Since hiring goals could be applied either inclusively or exclusively, whether the decree mandated appropriate "diagnostic goals that measure the efficacy of pool expansion techniques such as affirmative recruitment" was treated as a question of underlying intent. The *Shuford* goals did not require preferences for women, the court found, and would not permit jobs to be set-aside for specific groups. Because the goals played no role in the selection process, they served only to measure the effectiveness of the recruitment programs and to "red flag" those positions where women were unde-rrepresented. As such, the goals were found to be inclusive and lawful. *Shuford* has been cited with approval by several federal appellate courts. Most recently, two separate appellate panels affirmed consent decrees requiring public employers to devise race-conscious employment examinations so as to minimize any racially discriminatory impact on minority candidates. "[N]othing in *Adarand* requires the application of strict scrutiny to this sort of race consciousness."[43]

Other courts have disagreed, however, and applied strict scrutiny analysis to facially inclusive affirmative action programs. In *Monterey Mechanical Co. v. Wilson*,[44] the Ninth Circuit considered a California affirmative action statute that required bidders on state contracts either to subcontract a percentage of their work to female- and minority-owned businesses or to document a "good faith effort" to do so. The acknowledged low bidder in the case had been denied a contract with a state university for failure to achieve the mandated goal or to document its outreach efforts. The appeals court found that the statute treated classes unequally because a minority prime contractor could avoid the necessity of subcontracting or demonstrating good faith efforts simply by doing a percentage of the work itself, an option not available to other bidders. In addition, the statute was found to encourage quotas, even if it did not necessarily require them.

Meanwhile, *Messer v. Meno* challenged an affirmative action program involving goals, statistics, and reporting requirements within the Texas Education Agency (TEA).[45] In vacating summary judgment for TEA, the Fifth Circuit rejected any distinction between inclusive and exclusive affirmative action, holding that strict scrutiny applies to all governmental racial classifications. In *dicta*, the court noted that the "evidence ... strongly suggests recruitment was not the sole activity affected by the [affirmative action program], and that once an applicant met the minimum requirements for a position, TEA employees considered race or gender in employment decisions."[46] Although not disputing the applicability of strict scrutiny, Judge Garza warned in a concurring opinion that "the tone of the majority's decision ... will send the message out that affirmative action is, for all intents and purposes, dead in the Fifth Circuit."[47]

Similarly, in *Schurr v. Resort Int'l Hotel*,[48] the Third Circuit disapproved a casino's goal-oriented affirmative action plan, which had been applied to deny employment to a white light-and-sound technician in favor of an equally qualified black applicant, because it had been implemented "in [t]he absence of any reference to or showing of past or present discrimination in the casino industry." The employer argued that the affirmative action plan, and the Casino Control Commission regulations on which it was based, did not create racial preferences, but simply articulated goals aimed at recruiting members of minority groups and women. The court, however, concluded that the regulations "have the practical effect of encouraging (if not outright compelling) discriminatory hiring," particularly because Resorts International supervisors who made hiring decisions testified to a belief that they had to take race into account when filling a position, if a particular job category had a lower percentage of minority employees than the stated percentage goal for that category. There was no "meaningful distinction," the court found, between the casino's requirements and the minority participation goals for nongovernmental contractors, which the Ninth Circuit invalidated in *Bras v. California Public Utilities Commission*.[49] In *Bras,* the goals had the effect of putting a non-minority contractor on unequal footing in competing for business from Pacific Bell, which was subject to minority hiring goals formulated by the California Public Utility Commission pursuant to state law.

Another federal appellate court has applied strict judicial scrutiny as per *Adarand* to defeat equal employment opportunity regulations of the Federal Communications Commission (FCC) imposing affirmative minority outreach and recruitment obligations on applicants for radio broadcast licenses. In *Lutheran Church-Missouri Synod v. FCC*,[50] the D.C. Circuit ruling stemmed from a challenge by the NAACP to the hiring practices of a Lutheran Church organization which holds FCC licenses for two radio stations broadcasting from a seminary in Clayton, Missouri. Because of the stations' religious mission, the church has a "Lutheran hiring preference" requiring job applicants to possess "knowledge of Lutheran doctrine." The FCC imposes two basic requirements on radio stations: they must refrain from discriminating in employment for racial, ethnic, or gender-based reasons; and they must adopt an affirmative action program of targeted efforts to recruit, hire, and promote women and minorities. Acting on the NAACP complaint, the FCC ruled that the church's Lutheran hiring preference was too broad, and that while the stations had not discriminated, they violated agency regulation because of insufficient minority recruitment. The church was ordered to pay a $25,000 penalty and to submit reports every six months listing all job applicants and hires, along with the sex and race of each, as well as a statement of their efforts to recruit minorities.

A three judge appellate panel rejected FCC and Justice Department arguments that a more lenient standard of review than strict scrutiny should apply since the FCC regulations "stop[ped] short of establishing preferences, quotas, ... set-asides" and did not mandate race-conscious "hiring decisions." *Adarand* required "[a]ll governmental action based on race"—even when "the government's motivation to aid minorities can be thought 'benign'"—to be narrowly tailored to meet a compelling governmental interest. According to the court, by requiring a "formal analysis" by the employer of minority "underrepresentation" and "availability" statistics, the FCC regulations "extend beyond outreach efforts and certainly influence ultimate hiring decisions" because they "pressure stations to maintain a work force that mirrors the racial breakdown of the 'metropolitan statistical area.'" For this reason, it mattered not to the court "whether a government hiring program imposes hard quotas, soft quotas, or goals" since any such race-conscious technique "induces an employer to hire with an eye toward meeting a numerical target."

Rather than a remedy for past discrimination, the justification advanced by the government for the FCC program was to foster "diverse" programming content, an interest deemed "important" but not "compelling" by the appellate panel. Indeed, the diversity-of-programming rationale "makes no sense," said the judge, in the "intrastation" context where the FCC's "purported goal of making a single station all things to all people" contradicts "the reality of the radio market, where each station targets a particular segment: one pop, one country, one news radio, and so on." Nor could the FCC regulations be considered "narrowly tailored" because they affected the hiring of even low-level employees whose impact on programming was negligible. In conclusion, the judge observed:

> Perhaps this is illustrative as to just how much burden the term diversity has been asked to bear in the latter part of the 20th century in the United States. It appears to have been coined both as a permanent justification for policies seeking racial proportionality in all walks oflife ('affirmative action' had only a temporary remedial connotation) and as a synonym for proportional representation itself. It has, in our view, been used by the Commission in both ways. We therefore conclude that its EEO regulations are unconstitutional and cannot serve as a basis for its decision and order in this case.[51]

In a sequel, *Broadcasters Association v. FCC,*[52] the appeals court voided new FCC rules designed to achieve "broad outreach" in recruiting women and minorities for broadcasting careers. Broadcasters were given a choice between programs specified by the FCC and station-initiated outreach programs. If the station designed its own program, it had to report the race and sex of each applicant or person employed. But the regulations specified that a company's record in hiring women and minorities would not be a factor in the license renewal decision. The alternative approach was struck down, again because the recordkeeping and reporting of employment statistics were deemed a coercive and "powerful threat," almost certain to pressure companies to seek proportional representation of women and minorities. Moreover, the entire rule succumbed to the court's analysis—the offending portion deemed non-severable from the whole—perhaps limiting prospects for recasting FCC affirmative action efforts.

## MILITARY CASES

The U.S. military has traditionally enjoyed considerable deference from federal courts in decisions affecting military staffing and manpower needs. Nonetheless, challenges to Army and Air Force equal opportunity policies have triggered strict scrutiny of embedded racial classifications. In *Berkley v. United States,*[53] for example, discharged white male officers from the Air Force brought a Fifth Amendment equal protection class action challenging the basis for selecting officers for a reduction in force. The litigation centered on the written instruction from the Air Force Secretary concerning the evaluation of women and minority officers for that purpose. The memorandum noted that such individuals may have been disadvantaged in their careers by past societal attitudes and underutilization by the service. The trial court found no racial classification drawn by the memorandum, and was satisfied that it met minimal rational basis constitutional standards. However, the federal circuit reversed and remanded.[54] It found that strict scrutiny was triggered because the evaluation instruction provided for a different standard based on race and gender. The case was ultimately settled.[55]

In *Christian v. United States*,[56] the U.S. Court of Claims reviewed a U.S. Army policy establishing retention goals for minority and female officers twice considered, but passed over for promotion, who would otherwise have been subject to mandatory early retirement. The percentage of minorities and women to be retired was set by a special Army memorandum, which established different evaluation standards for minorities and women than officers in general, ostensibly due to possible past personal or institutional discrimination.

The claims court found that whether the Army program was viewed as a "goal," "quota," or otherwise, the special procedures "pressure[d]" review board members "into making racially tainted decisions," thus amounting to "a racial classification subject to strict scrutiny." It also found that the purposes put forward by the government in defense of the policy fell short of "compelling" for several reasons. First, the Army's desire to project a "perception" of equal opportunity and to address the problem of "possible past discrimination" in previous training and assignments was not equivalent to "finding that a particular minority officer was in fact discriminated against." Further undermining any remedial justification for the policy was its focus on issues of "past personal discrimination"—in promotions, assignments, and military school attendance—affecting minority members of the Army, in general, rather than previous biased acts of the retirement board, the entity responsible for implementing the minority retention program. In this respect, the court likened the policy to remedies for "societal discrimination," which *Croson* and *Adarand* rejected as a "compelling" governmental interest. The Army's plan was found to address mere "statistical disparities" in minority retention rates, whatever the cause, rather than proven "present effects of past discrimination," the only constitutional justification for racial affirmative action.[57]

The Army procedure failed the additional constitutional requirement that affirmative action measures be "narrowly tailored." The minority retention goal was not the "least intrusive means" to remedy discrimination by the Army in promotions. Promotion or recruitment goals would accomplish the same purpose by "more exact connection" to identified institutional discrimination with less burden on affected nonminority officers. Moreover, the policy was of indefinite duration, with no built-in time limitation, and no race-neutral alternatives were attempted by the government before implementing its affirmative action plan. One alternative suggested by the court was to increase educational and training opportunities for all officers from underprivileged backgrounds, whatever their race. This, it was contended, would expand the pool of minorities eligible for promotion and address the Army's concern for societal discrimination without employing a suspect classification. The government successfully appealed the remedy portion of the Court of Claims decree, which required reinstatement and backpay of involuntarily retired white male officers.[58] But the lower court's threshold determination that the minority retention program violated equal protection was neither appealed to nor addressed by the Federal Circuit.

Similarly, in a legal action by a white officer who was twice denied promotion to full colonel in 1996 and 1997, *Saunders v. White*,[59] a federal district court ruled the Army's equal opportunity promotion process in use at the time unconstitutional. The Army's written instruction to promotion boards required that the possibility of personal or institutional discrimination be taken into account when evaluating the promotion files of women and minority officers—both in initial evaluation and any review or revote—and urged that the percentages promoted from these groups match their proportion in the applicant pool. Because Army promotion selection statistics for more than two decades demonstrated that minorities and women were promoted at virtually the same rate as whites—if not slightly higher—the judge found that there was no demonstrable record of discrimination to justify the Army's consideration of race or gender in its promotion policy. The fatal defect in the Army policy was summed up by the district court: "Nowhere in the Memorandum are selection board officers obliged to consider the possibility of past discrimination for non-Nurse Corps males, whites, or any other group for which there is not an equal opportunity selection goal. Thus, the Memorandum instructs selection board members to, for example, account for an Hispanic applicant's 'past personal or institutional discrimination,' but not to account for a white applicant's past discrimination. This undeniably establishes a preference in favor of one race or gender over another, and therefore is unconstitutional."[60]

## End Notes

[1] See e.g. Green v. County Bd., 391 U.S. 430 (1968); Swann v. Bd. of Educ., 402 U.S. 1 (1971); Keyes v. Denver School District, 413 U.S. 189 (1973). See also, CRS Report RL30410, *Affirmative Action and Diversity in Public Education: Legal Developments*, by Jody Feder.

[2] 42 U.S.C. §§ 2000e et seq.

[3] Id. at § 2000e-5(g).

[4] Section 717 of the 1972 Amendments to Title VII of the 1964 Civil Rights Act empowers the EEOC to enforce nondiscrimination policy in federal employment by "necessary and appropriate" rules, regulations, and orders and through "appropriate remedies, including reinstatement or hiring of employees, with or without backpay." Id. at § 2000e-16(b). Each federal department and agency, in turn, is required to prepare annually a "national and regional equal employment opportunity plan" for submission to the EEOC as part of "an affirmative program of equal employment opportunity for all ... employees and applicants for employment." Id. at § 2000e-16(b)(1). Section 717 was reinforced in 1978 when Congress enacted major federal civil service reforms, including a mandate for immediate development of a "minority recruitment program" designed to eliminate "underrepresentation" of minority groups in federal agency employment. 5 U.S.C. § 7201. The EEOC and Office of Personnel Management have issued rules to guide implementation and monitoring of minority recruitment programs by individual federal agencies. Among various other specified requirements, each agency plan "must include annual specific determinations of underrepresentation for each group and must be accompanied by quantifiable indices by which progress toward eliminating underrepresentation can be measured." 5 C.F.R. § 720.205(b).

[5] See 41 C.F.R. §§ 60-1 to 999.

[6] United Steelworkers v. Weber, 443 U.S. 193 (1979).

[7] Local 28 Sheet Metal Workers v. EEOC, 478 U.S. 421 (1986).

[8] United States v. Paradise, 480 U.S. 149 (1987); Johnson v. Transp. Agency, 480 U.S. 616 (1987).

[9] 478 U.S. 421 (1986); 480 U.S. 149 (1987).

[10] 476 U.S. 267 (1986).

[11] 443 U.S. 193 (1979).

[12] In this regard the Court emphasized: "The plan does not require the discharge of white workers and their replacement with new black hires. Nor does the plan create an absolute bar to advancement of white employees; half of those trained in the program will be white. Moreover, the plan is a temporary measure; it is not intended to maintain racial balance, but simply to eliminate manifest racial imbalance. Preferential selection of craft trainees at the ... plant will end as soon as the percentage of black skilled craft workers in the ... plant approximates the percentage of blacks in the local labor force." Id. at 208-09.

[13] 480 U.S. 792 (1973).

[14] Regents of the Univ. of California v. Bakke, 438 U.S. 265 (1978).

[15] Id. at 636 (citing Sheet Metal Workers v. EEOC, 478 U.S. 421, 495 (O'Connor, J., concurring in part and dissenting in part). Justice Stevens concurred that the plan was consistent with *Weber* and Justice O'Connor, in a separate concurrence, provided a sixth vote for the judgment. In her opinion, however, to support a voluntary affirmative action plan, there should be "a statistical disparity sufficient to support a prima facie claim under Title VII by the employee beneficiaries of the affirmative action.... " Equal Protection standards, not Title VII, should govern public employee cases, and she was critical of the majority for

providing inadequate guidance as to the statistical imbalance standard. But because there were no women in skilled craft positions, and gender was only a plus factor, either standard was satisfied here.

[16] Patrolmen's Benevolent Assoc. v. City of New York, 310 F.3d 43, 52 (2002) (quoting Barhold v. Rodriguez, 863 F.2d 233, 238 (2d Cir. 1988)); Reynolds v. City of Chicago, 296 F.3d 524 (7th Cir. 2002). See also Cotter v. City of Boston, 323 F.3d 160, 172 n. 10 (1st Cir. 2003)(declining to address question of compelling interest but expressing sympathy for "the argument that communities place more trust in a diverse police force and that the resulting trust reduces crime rates and improves policing"); Wittmer v. Peters, 87 F. 3d 916 (7th Cir. 1996)(consideration of race permitted in promoting black corrections officer to supervisor because prison could not accomplish its "mission of pacification and reformation" of predominantly black inmates with nearly all white staff). But see Lomack v. City of Newark, 463 F.3d 303 (3d Cir. 2006) (city policy designed to eliminate single-race fire companies by involuntarily transferring firefighters to different companies solely on the basis of race violated the Equal Protection Clause).

[17] In *Grutter v. Bollinger*, 539 U.S. 506 (2003), a 5 to 4 majority of the Justices held that the University of Michigan Law School had a "compelling" interest in the "educational benefits that flow from a diverse student body," which justified its race-based efforts to assemble a "critical mass" of "underrepresented" minority students. For more information, see CRS Report RL30410, *Affirmative Action and Diversity in Public Education: Legal Developments*, by Jody Feder.

[18] 352 F.3d 1111 (7th Cir. 2003), cert. denied 541 U.S. 1074 (U.S. 2004).

[19] 129 S. Ct. 2658 (2009).

[20] For more information on the *Ricci* decision, see CRS Report R40697, *Race Discrimination and the Supreme Court: A Legal Analysis of Ricci v. DeStefano*, by Jody Feder.

[21] 488 U.S. 469 (1989)(rejecting a local government's effort to promote public contracting opportunities for minority entrepreneurs).

[22] E.g. Majeske v. City of Chicago, 218 F.3d 816 (7th Cir. 2000)(city's affirmative action plan lawful because it remedies past discrimination and was narrowly tailored); McNamara v. City of Chicago, 138 F.3d 1219, 1223-24 (7th Cir. 1998)(stating that raw statistics do not prove intentional discrimination, but also finding that defendant had presented strong basis in evidence of need to remedy discrimination, through combination of statistics, anecdotal evidence, and judicial findings); Boston Police Superior Officers Fed'n, 147 F.3d 13, (1st Cir. 1998)(documentary evidence in relation to earlier consent decree supported preferential promotion of black officer to rank of lieutenant). But cf. Crumpton v. Bridgeport Educ. Ass'n, 993 F.2d 1023 (2d Cir. 1993)(refusing to equate parties' stipulations as to existence of discrimination with judicial determination that such discrimination existed); Reynolds v. Roberts, 202 F.3d 1303 (11th Cir. 2000)(consent decree did not establish that state transportation department had discriminated against black employees).

[23] See "Backdraft, Courts are Lifting Decades-Old Consent Decrees Requiring Affirmative Action," 86 A.B.A.J. 48 (April 2000).

[24] 515 U.S. 200 (1995)(applying "strict scrutiny" to a federal transportation program of financial incentives for prime contractors who subcontracted to firms owned by racial minorities and ruling that all "racial classifications" by government at any level must be justified by a "compelling governmental interest" and "narrowly tailored" to that end).

[25] In re Birmingham Reverse Discrimination Employment Litig., 20 F.3d 1525 (11th Cir. 1994). See also Thigpen v. Bibb County Ga., Sheriff's Dep't, 223 F.3d 1231 (11th Cir. 2000)(*Croson* controlled white police officers' § 1983 action against sheriff's department,

challenging constitutionality of consent decree, adopted to settle prior race discrimination action, requiring that 50% of all annual promotions be awarded to black officers).

[26] See Cotter v. City of Boston, 73 F. Supp. 2d 62 (D.Mass. 1999), vacated and remanded, 219 F.3d 31 (lst Cir. 2000).

[27] 150 F.3d 438 (5th Cir. 1998), cert. denied, 526 U.S. 1046 (1999).

[28] Id. at 440.

[29] 31 F.3d 1548 (11th Cir. 1994).

[30] Id. at 1577. In addition, the court noted: "Once a valid selection procedure is in place for a particular position, neither the City or the Board may continue to certify, hire, or promote according to a race-conscious 'goal' absent proof of ongoing racial discrimination, or of lingering effects of past racial discrimination, with respect to that position. Under no circumstances may the City hire or promote, or the Board certify, candidates who are demonstrably less qualified than other candidates, based on the results of valid, job-related selection procedures, unless the district court finds that such appointments are necessary to cure employment discrimination by the City or Board." Id.

[31] 993 F.2d 1072 (4th Cir. 1993).

[32] E.g. Alexander v. Estepp, 95 F.3d 312, 316 (4th Cir. 1996)("The program is not narrowly tailored because means less drastic than outright racial classification were available to department officials"; Middleton v. City of Flint, 92 F.3d 396, 410-11 (6th Cir. 1996)(rejecting race-conscious promotion plan because, inter alia, the City had successfully used "less drastic, alternative ways" to increase percentage of minority police officers); Boston Police Superior Officers Fed'n v. City of Boston, 147 F.3d 13, 25 (1st Cir. 1998)(holding that one-time affirmative action promotion was narrowly tailored because race-neutral measures "would not provide a timely remedy.")

[33] Detroit Police Officers Ass'n v. Young, 989 F.2d 225, 228 (6th Cir. 1993).

[34] Lalla v. City of New Orleans, 1999 U.S. Dist. LEXIS 3281 (D. La. 1999)("gross statistical disparities" between racial composition of fire department and community population did not establish "strong basis in evidence" for racial hiring preference absent showing that black applicants were rejected as "much higher" rate than whites); Ashton v. City of Memphis, 49 F. Supp.2d 1051 (W.D.Tenn. 1999)(testimony of expert for city overstated number of blacks in qualified labor pool because wrong age group was considered, and it disregarded both the level of minority group interest and relatively higher rates of criminal convictions among blacks, disqualifying factors for police officers); Aiken v. City of Memphis, 37 F.3d 1155 (6th Cir. 1994)(promotion goals set by consent decree were problematic because they were tied to goals for hiring black officers which were, in turn, based on the minority population of the undifferentiated labor force).

[35] United States v. City of Miami, 115 F.3d 870 (11th Cir. 1997)(report of city's expert on underrepresentation of women and minorities as firefighters lacked probative value where it was based on general census data rather than proper comparisons between minority composition of department and relevant labor market); Ashton, supra n. 33 at 1065 (district court "troubled" by city's long-term operation under consent decrees—some fourteen years).

[36] E.g. North State Law Enforcement Officers Ass'n v. Charlotte-Mecklenburg Police Dep't., 862 F. Supp. 1445 (W.D.N.C. 1994).

[37] E.g. Crumpton v. Bridgeport Educ. Ass'n, 993 F.2d 1023, 1031 (2d Cir. 1993)(finding preferential lay-off policy too burdensome on nonminorities).

[38] Sussman v. Tanoue, 39 F.Supp.2d 13, 24 (D.D.C. 1999)(quoting United States v. New Hampshire, 539 F.2d 277, 280 (1st Cir. 1976).

[39] See, e.g., Allen v. Alabama State Bd. of Educ., 164 F.3d 1347, 1352 (11th Cir. 1999)(racially conscious outreach efforts to broaden applicant pool not subject to strict scrutiny), vacated 216 F.3d 1263 (11th Cir. 2000); Duffy v. Wolle, 123 F.3d 1026, 1038-39 (8th Cir. 1997)("An employer's affirmative efforts to recruit female and minority applicants does not constitute discrimination."); Ensley Branch, NAACP, supra n. 30, at p. 1571 (describing efforts to actively encourage Blacks to apply for jobs, including waivers of application fees, as "race-neutral"); Billish v. City of Chicago, 962 F.2d 1269, 1290 (7th Cir. 1992)(describing aggressive recruiting as "race-neutral procedures") rev'd on other grounds, 989 F.2d 890 (7th Cir.1993)(en banc).

[40] 897 F. Supp. 1535 (M.D.Ala. 1995).

[41] Id. at 1552.

[42] Id. at 1553.

[43] Allen v. Alabama State Bd. of Educ., supra n. 40, at p. 1353 (affirming consent decree requiring that school board develop teacher certification exam that minimizes racially discriminatory impact); Hayden v. County of Nassau, 180 F.3d 42, 49(2d Cir. 1999) ("[A]lthough Nassau County was necessarily conscious of race in designing its entrance exam [for police officer candidates], it treated all persons equally in the administration of the exam.").

[44] 125 F.3d 702 (9th Cir. 1997), reh'g en banc denied, 138 F.3d 1270 (9th Cir. 1998).

[45] 130 F.3d 130 (5th Cir. 1997).

[46] Id. at 139.

[47] Id. at 141 (Garza J., concurring).

[48] 196 F.3d 486 (3d Cir. 1999)

[49] 59 F.3d 869 (9th Cir. 1995), cert. denied, 516 U.S. 1984 (1996).

[50] 141 F.3d 344 (D.C.Cir. 1998).

[51] Id. at 356.

[52] 236 F.3d 13 (D.C.Cir. 2001).

[53] 48 Fed. Cl. 361 (Fed. Cl. 2000).

[54] Berkley v. United States, 287 F.3d 1076 (Fed. Cir. 2002).

[55] Berkley v. United States, 59 Fed. Cl. 675 (Fed. Cl. 2004).

[56] 46 Fed. Cl. 793 (2000).

[57] See also Sirmans v. Brownlee, 346 F.Supp.2d 56 (D.D.C. 2004).

[58] Christian v. United States, 337 F.3d 1338 (Fed. Cir. 2003).

[59] 191 F.Supp.2d 95 (D.D.C. 2002).

[60] Id at 101.

In: Affirmative Action and Preferential Treatment ISBN: 978-1-62257-465-0
Editors: P. L. Medina and J. E. Patel 

*Chapter 4*

# AFFIRMATIVE ACTION AND DIVERSITY IN PUBLIC EDUCATION: LEGAL DEVELOPMENTS*

***Jody Feder***

## SUMMARY

Over a quarter century after the Supreme Court ruling in *Regents of the University of California v. Bakke*, the diversity rationale for affirmative action in public education remains a topic of political and legal controversy. Many colleges and universities have implemented affirmative action policies not only to remedy past discrimination, but also to achieve a racially and ethnically diverse student body or faculty. Justice Powell, in his opinion for the *Bakke* Court, stated that the attainment of a diverse student body is "a constitutionally permissible goal for an institution of higher education," noting that "[t]he atmosphere of 'speculation, experiment, and creation' so essential to the quality of higher education is widely believed to be promoted by a diverse student body." In subsequent years, however, federal courts began to question the Powell rationale, unsettling expectations about the constitutionality of diversity-based affirmative action in educational admissions and faculty hiring.

---

* This is an edited, reformatted and augmented version of Congressional Research Service, Publication No. RL30410, dated January 30, 2009.

After a series of conflicting lower court rulings were issued regarding the use of race to promote a diverse student body, the Supreme Court agreed to review the race-conscious admissions policies used by the undergraduate and law school admissions programs at the University of Michigan. In *Grutter v. Bollinger*, a 5 to 4 majority of the Justices held that the University Law School had a "compelling" interest in the "educational benefits that flow from a diverse student body," which justified its race-based efforts to assemble a "critical mass" of "underrepresented" minority students. But in the companion decision, *Gratz v. Bollinger*, six Justices decided that the University's policy of awarding "racial bonus points" to minority applicants was not "narrowly tailored" enough to pass constitutional scrutiny. The decisions resolved, for the time being, the doctrinal muddle left in *Bakke*'s wake. And because the Court's constitutional holdings translate to the private sector under the federal civil rights laws, nonpublic schools, colleges, and universities are likewise affected.

Although the *Grutter* and *Gratz* decisions settled the question of whether race-based policies to promote diversity in higher education are ever constitutionally acceptable, the decisions did not address whether diversity is a permissible goal in the elementary and secondary educational setting. To resolve this question, the Supreme Court agreed to review two cases that involve the use of race to maintain racially diverse public schools and to avoid racial segregation. In a consolidated ruling in *Parents Involved in Community Schools v. Seattle School District No. 1*, the Court struck down the Seattle and Louisville school plans at issue, holding that they violated the equal protection guarantee of the Fourteenth Amendment.

## I. Introduction

Over a quarter century after the Supreme Court ruling in *Regents of the University of California v. Bakke*,[1] the diversity rationale for affirmative action in public education remains a topic of political and legal controversy. Many colleges and universities have implemented affirmative action policies not only to remedy past discrimination, but also to achieve a racially and ethnically diverse student body or faculty. Justice Powell, in his opinion for the *Bakke* Court, stated that the attainment of a diverse student body is "a constitutionally permissible goal for an institution of higher education," noting that "[t]he atmosphere of 'speculation, experiment, and creation' so essential to the quality of higher education is widely believed to be promoted by a diverse student body."

In subsequent years, however, federal courts began to question the Powell rationale, unsettling expectations about the constitutionality of diversity-based affirmative action in educational admissions and faculty hiring decisions. In striking down the admissions process at the University of Texas School of Law, the Fifth Circuit in *Hopwood v. Texas* concluded that any use of race in the admissions process was forbidden by the Constitution.[2] Reverberations of the 1996 *Hopwood* opinion are apparent in several subsequent cases, which voided "race conscious" policies maintained by institutions of higher education, as well as public elementary and secondary schools. Some judges avoided resolving the precedential effect of Justice Powell's opinion by deciding the case on "narrow tailoring"or other grounds not dependent on the constitutional status of student diversity as a compelling state interest.[3] But, in *Johnson v. Board of Regents*, the Eleventh Circuit sided with *Hopwood* by rejecting diversity as constitutional justification for a numerical "racial bonus" awarded minority freshman applicants to the University of Georgia. A circuit court conflict was created when the Ninth Circuit relied on *Bakke* to uphold an affirmative action admissions policy to the University of Washington Law School that made extensive use of race-based factors. *Smith v. University of Washington* was the first federal appeals court to rely on Justice Powell's decision as binding precedent on the issue.[4]

The judicial divide over *Bakke*'s legacy was vividly underscored by a pair of separate trial court decisions, one upholding for diversity reasons the race-based undergraduate admissions policy of the University of Michigan,[5] the other voiding a special minority law school admissions program at the same institution.[6] Restoring a degree of clarity to the law, the U.S. Supreme Court concluded its 2002-03 term with rulings in the Michigan cases. In *Grutter v. Bollinger*,[7] a 5 to 4 majority of the Justices held that the University Law School had a "compelling" interest in the "educational benefits that flow from a diverse student body," which justified its consideration of race in admissions to assemble a "critical mass" of "underrepresented" minority students. But in a companion decision, *Gratz v. Bollinger*,[8] six Justices decided that the University's policy of awarding "racial bonus points" to minority applicants was not "narrowly tailored" enough to pass constitutional scrutiny.

Although the *Grutter* and *Gratz* decisions settled the question of whether race-based policies to promote diversity in higher education are ever constitutionally acceptable, the decisions did not address whether diversity is a permissible goal in the elementary and secondary educational setting. To resolve this question, the Supreme Court agreed to review two cases that involved the use of race to maintain racially diverse public schools. The cases were *Meredith v. Jefferson County Board of Education*—formerly *MacFarland v. Jefferson County Public Schools*—and *Parents Involved in Community Schools v. Seattle School District No. 1*.[9] In *Parents Involved in Community Schools v. Seattle School District No. 1*, a consolidated ruling that resolved both cases, the Court ultimately struck down the school plans at issue, holding that they violated the equal protection guarantee of the Fourteenth Amendment.[10]

The first part of this report briefly reviews the judicial evolution of race-based affirmative action, particularly in relation to public education. Recent rulings challenging the use of race-conscious admissions and hiring practices by public educational institutions are then considered for their implications on the future development of affirmative action law.

## II. HISTORICAL BACKGROUND

The origins of affirmative action law may be traced to the early 1960's as first the Warren, and then the Burger Court, grappled with the seemingly intractable problem of racial segregation in the nation's public schools. Judicial rulings from this period recognized an "affirmative duty," cast upon local school boards by the Equal Protection Clause, to desegregate formerly "dual school" systems and to eliminate "root and branch" the last "vestiges" of state-enforced segregation.[11] These holdings ushered in a two decade era of "massive" desegregation—first in the South, and later the urban North—marked by federal desegregation orders frequently requiring drastic reconfiguration of school attendance patterns along racial lines and extensive student transportation schemes. School districts across the nation operating under these decrees have since sought to be declared in compliance with constitutional requirements in order to gain release from federal intervention. The Supreme Court eventually responded by holding that judicial control of a school system previously found guilty of intentional segregation should be relinquished if, looking to all aspects of school operations, it appears that the district has complied with desegregation requirements in "good faith" for a "reasonable period of time" and has eliminated "vestiges" of past discrimination "to the extent practicable."[12]

A statutory framework for affirmative action in employment and education was enacted by the Civil Rights Act of 1964. Public and private employers with 15 or more employees are subject to a comprehensive code of equal employment opportunity regulations under Title VII of the 1964 Act.

The Title VII remedial scheme rests largely on judicial power to order monetary damages and injunctive relief, including "such affirmative action as may be appropriate,"[13] to make discrimination victims whole. Except as may be imposed by court order or consent decree to remedy past discrimination, however, there is no general statutory obligation on employers to adopt affirmative action remedies. But the Equal Employment Opportunity Commission (EEOC) has issued guidelines to protect employers and unions from charges of "reverse discrimination" when they voluntarily take action to correct the effects of past discrimination.[14]

The term "affirmative action" resurfaced in federal regulations construing the 1964 Act's Title VI, which prohibits racial or ethnic discrimination in all federally assisted "programs" and activities,[15] including public or private educational institutions. The Office of Civil Rights of the Department of Education interpreted Title VI to require schools and colleges to take affirmative action to overcome the effects of past discrimination and to encourage "voluntary affirmative action to attain a diverse student body."[16] Another Title VI regulation permits a college or university to take racial or national origin into account when awarding financial aid if the aid is necessary to overcome effects of past institutional discrimination.[17] Affirmative action in higher education was before the Congress in 1998, when the full House defeated a bill to prohibit federal aid to colleges and universities that consider race, ethnicity, or sex in the admission process.

The *Bakke* ruling in 1978 launched the contemporary constitutional debate over state-sponsored affirmative action. A "notable lack of unanimity" was evident from the six separate opinions filed in that case. One four-Justice plurality in *Bakke* voted to strike down as a violation of Title VI a special admissions program of the University of California at Davis medical school which set-aside sixteen of one hundred positions in each incoming class for minority students, where the institution itself was not shown to have discriminated in the past. Another bloc of four Justices argued that racial classifications designed to further remedial purposes were foreclosed neither by the Constitution nor the Civil Rights Act and would have upheld the minority admissions quota. Justice Powell added a fifth vote to each camp by condemning the Davis program on equal protection grounds while endorsing the nonexclusive consideration of race as an admissions criterion to foster student diversity.

In Justice Powell's view, neither the state's asserted interest in remedying "societal discrimination," nor of providing "role models" for minority students was sufficiently "compelling" to warrant the use of a "suspect" racial classification in the admission process. But the attainment of a "diverse student body" was, for Justice Powell, "clearly a permissible goal for an institution of higher education" since diversity of minority viewpoints furthered "academic freedom," a "special concern of the First Amendment."[18] Accordingly, race could be considered by a university as a "plus" or "one element of a range of factors"—even if it "tipped the scale" among qualified applicants—as long as it "did not insulate the individual from comparison with all the other candidates for the available seats."[19] The "quota" in *Bakke* was infirm, however, since it defined diversity only in racial terms and absolutely excluded non-minorities from a given number of seats. By two 5-to-4 votes, therefore, the Supreme Court affirmed the lower court order admitting Bakke but reversed the judicial ban on consideration of race in admissions.

*Bakke* was followed by *Wygant v. Jackson Board of Education*,[20] where a divided Court ruled unconstitutional the provision of a collective bargaining agreement that protected minority public school teachers from layoff at the expense of more senior white faculty members. While holding the specific layoff preference for minority teachers unconstitutional, seven *Wygant* Justices seemed to agree in principle that a governmental employer is not prohibited by the Equal Protection Clause from all race-conscious affirmative action to remedy its own past discrimination. Another series of decisions approved of congressionally mandated racial preferences to allocate the benefits of contracts on federally sponsored public works projects,[21] and in the design of certain broadcast licensing schemes,[22] while condemning similar actions taken by local governmental entities to promote public contracting opportunities for minority entrepreneurs.[23] However, in each of these cases, the Justices failed to achieve a consensus on most issues, with bare majorities, pluralities, or—as in *Bakke*—a single Justice, determining the "law" of the case.

By the mid-1980's, the Supreme Court had approved the temporary remedial use of race- or gender-conscious selection criteria by private employers under Title VII of the 1964 Civil Rights Act.[24] These measures were deemed a proper remedy for "manifest racial imbalance" in "traditionally segregated" job categories, if voluntarily adopted by the employer,[25] or for entrenched patterns of "egregious and longstanding" discrimination by the employer, if imposed by judicial decree.[26] In either circumstance, however, the Court required proof of remedial justification rooted in the employer's own past discrimination and its persistent workplace effects. Thus, a "firm basis" in evidence, as revealed by a "manifest imbalance"—or "historic," "persistent," and "egregious" underrepresentation—of minorities or women in affected job categories was deemed an essential predicate to preferential affirmative action.

Second, but of equal importance, all racial preferences in employment were to be judged in terms of their adverse impact on "identifiable" non-minority group members. Remedies that protected minorities from layoff, for example, were most suspect and unlikely to pass legal or constitutional muster if they displaced more senior white workers. But the consideration of race or gender as a "plus" factor in employment decisions, when it did not unduly hinder or "trammel" the "legitimate expectations" of non-minority employees, won ready judicial acceptance.[27] Affirmative action preferences, however, had to be sufficiently flexible, temporary in duration, and "narrowly tailored" to avoid becoming rigid "quotas."

Not until 1989, however, did a majority of the Justices resolve the proper constitutional standard for review of governmental classifications by race enacted for a remedial or other "benign" legislative purpose. Disputes prior to *City of Richmond v. J.A. Croson*[28] yielded divergent views as to whether state affirmative action measures for the benefit of racial minorities were subject to the same "strict scrutiny" as applied to "invidious" racial discrimination under the Equal Protection Clause, an "intermediate" standard resembling the test for gender-based classifications, or simple rationality. In *Croson*, a 5 to 4 majority settled on strict scrutiny to invalidate a 30% set-aside of city contracts for minority-owned businesses because the program was not "narrowly tailored" to a "compelling" governmental interest. While "race-conscious" remedies could be legislated in response to proven past discrimination by the affected governmental entities, "racial balancing" untailored to "specific" and "identified" evidence of minority exclusion was impermissible. *Croson* suggested, however, that because of its unique equal protection enforcement authority, a constitutional standard more tolerant of racial line-drawing may apply to Congress. This conclusion was reinforced a year later when, in *Metro Broadcasting, Inc. v. FCC*,[29] the Court upheld certain minority broadcast licensing schemes approved by Congress to promote the "important" governmental interest in "broadcast diversity."

The two-tiered approach to equal protection analysis of governmental affirmative action was short-lived. In *Adarand Constructors, Inc. v. Pena,*[30] the Court applied "strict scrutiny" to a federal transportation program of financial incentives for prime contractors who subcontracted to firms owned by "socially and economically disadvantaged individuals," defined so as to prefer members of designated racial minorities. Although the Court refrained from deciding the constitutional merits of the particular program before it, and remanded for further proceedings below, it determined that all "racial classifications" by government at any level must be justified by a "compelling governmental interest" and "narrowly tailored" to that end. But the majority opinion sought to "dispel the notion" that "strict scrutiny is `strict in theory, but fatal in fact,'" by acknowledging a role for Congress as architect of remedies for discrimination nationwide. "The unhappy persistence of both the practices and lingering effects of racial discrimination against minorities in this country is an unfortunate reality, and the government is not disqualified from acting in response to it." No further guidance is provided, however, as to the scope of remedial power remaining in congressional hands, or of the conditions required for its exercise. Bottom line, *Adarand* suggests that racial preferences in federal law or policy are a remedy of last resort and must be adequately justified and narrowly drawn to pass constitutional muster.

# III. Recent Legal Developments

## Student Diversity in Higher Education Admissions

The emphasis in *Adarand* on past discrimination prompted a surge in judicial challenges to educational diversity as an independent justification for student and faculty affirmative action. The notion that diversity could rise to the level of a compelling interest in the educational setting sprang a quarter century ago from Justice Powell's opinion in the *Bakke* case. While concluding that a state medical school could not set-aside a certain number of seats for minority applicants, Justice Powell opined that a diverse student body may serve educators' legitimate interest in promoting the "robust" exchange of ideas. He cautioned, however, that "[t]he diversity that furthers a compelling state interest encompasses a far broader array of qualifications and characteristics of which ethnic origin is but a single though important element."[31]

Justice Powell split the difference between two four-Justice pluralities in *Bakke*. One camp, led by Justice Stevens, struck down the admissions quota on statutory civil rights grounds. Another led by Justice Brennan would have upheld the medical school's policy as a remedy for societal discrimination. Justice Powell held the "dual admissions" procedure to be unconstitutional, and ordered Bakke's admission. But, he concluded, that the state's interest in educational diversity could warrant consideration of students' race in certain circumstances. For Justice Powell, a diverse student body fostered the "robust" exchange of ideas and academic freedom deserving of constitutional protection.

Justice Powell's theory of diversity as a compelling governmental interest did not turn on race alone. He pointed with approval to the "Harvard Plan," which defined diversity in terms of a broad array of factors and characteristics. Thus, an applicant's race could be deemed a "plus" factor. It was considered on a par with personal talents, leadership qualities, family background, or any other factor contributing to a diverse student body. However, the race of a candidate could not be the "sole" or "determinative" factor. No other Justice joined in the Powell opinion.

Although Justice Powell's opinion announced the judgment of the Court, no other *Bakke* Justices joined him on that point. Justice Powell ruled the "dual admission program" at issue to be unconstitutional and the white male plaintiff entitled to admission, while four other Justices reached the same result on statutory rather than constitutional grounds. Another four Justice plurality concluded that the challenged policy was lawful, but agreed with Justice Powell that the state court had erred by holding that an applicant's race could never be taken into account. Only Justice Powell, therefore, expressed the view that the attainment of a diverse student body could be a compelling state interest.

For nearly two decades, colleges and universities relied on the Powell opinion in *Bakke* to support race-conscious student diversity policies. Consideration of race in admissions, which took various forms, stood pretty much unchallenged until *Hopwood v. State of Texas*.[32] A panel of the Fifth Circuit repudiated the Powell diversity rationale when it voided a special admission program of the University of Texas law school. Unlike *Bakke*, the Texas program entailed no explicit racial quota. But, in other respects, it was a classic dual track system: one standard for blacks and Hispanics, another for everyone else, and cutoff scores for minorities were lower. The Powell opinion was not binding precedent, the *Hopwood* panel ruled, since it was not joined by any other justice. Thus, race could be considered in admissions only to remedy past discrimination by the law school itself, which was not shown in *Hopwood*.

Several other federal circuit courts, besides the Sixth Circuit in the Michigan case, looked at race-based college admissions after *Bakke*. *Johnson v. Board of Regents*[33] struck down the award of "racial bonus" points to minority students as one of 12 factors—academic and nonacademic—considered for freshman admissions to the University of Georgia. The Eleventh Circuit majority was skeptical of the Powell opinion but did not take a stand on the diversity issue. Instead, the program failed the second requirement of strict scrutiny. It was not "narrowly tailored." That is, it "mechanically awards an arbitrary 'diversity' bonus to each and every non-white applicant at a decisive stage in the admissions process." At the same time, the policy arbitrarily limited the number of nonracial factors that could be considered, all at the expense of white applicants, even those whose social or economic background and personal traits would promote "experiential" diversity. On the other hand, the Ninth Circuit upheld the minority law school admissions program at the University of Washington on the basis of *Bakke*. The appeals court in *Smith v. University of Washington Law School*[34] concluded that the four Brennan Justices who approved of the racial quota in *Bakke* "would have embraced [the diversity rationale] if need be." Justice Powell's opinion thus became the "narrowest footing" for approval of race in admission and was the "holding" of *Bakke*.

Post-*Bakke* appeals courts, guided by *Marks v. United States*,[35] sliced and diced the various opinions in *Bakke* to come up with a controlling rationale. In *Marks*, the Supreme Court ruled that when a majority of Justices are unable to agree on a controlling rationale, the holding of the Court is the position of those Justices concurring in the judgment on the narrowest grounds. The pro-diversity circuits concluded that the Powell opinion approving race as a "plus" factor was narrower than the Brennan rationale, which would have upheld the race quota in *Bakke* on a societal discrimination theory. The opposing circuits had generally reasoned otherwise or concluded that the competing *Bakke* opinions defy rational comparison so that absent a majority consensus, the Powell opinion was without controlling weight. In no way bound by *Bakke*, Supreme Court review of the Michigan cases augured fundamental reexamination of issues raised by that earlier precedent.

## Background in the University of Michigan Admissions Cases

The judicial divide over the student diversity policies deepened with the Michigan cases. One federal district court in *Grutter* originally struck down the student diversity policy of the University of Michigan Law School, while another judge upheld a procedure awarding points to "underrepresented minority" applicants to the undergraduate school.[36] Based on *Bakke*, the Sixth Circuit reversed *Grutter* and permitted the Law School to consider race in admissions.[37] The Supreme Court granted *certiorari* in *Grutter* and agreed to review *Gratz* prior to judgment by the Sixth Circuit.

Undergraduate admission to the University of Michigan had been based on a point system or "student selection index." A total possible 150 points could be awarded for factors, academic and otherwise, that made up the selection index. Academic factors accounted for up to 110 points, including 12 for standardized test performance. By comparison, 20 points could be awarded for one, but only one, of the following: membership in an underrepresented minority group, socioeconomic disadvantage, or athletics. Applicants could receive one to four points for "legacy" or alumni relationships, three points for personal essay, five points for community leadership and service, six points for in-state residency, etc. In practice, students at the extremes of academic performance were typically admitted or rejected on that basis alone. But for the middle range of qualified applicants, these other factors were often determinative. Finally, counselors could "flag" applications for review by the Admissions Review Committee, where any factor important to the freshman class composition—race included—was not adequately reflected in the selection index score.

In upholding this policy, the district court in *Gratz* found that *Bakke* and the University's own evidence demonstrating the educational benefits of racial and ethnic diversity established a compelling state interest. And the award of 20 points for minority status was not a "quota" or "dual track" system, as in *Bakke*, but only a "plus factor," to be weighed against others in the selection process. Thus, the constitutional demand for "narrow tailoring" was satisfied. The *Gratz* district court also concluded that "vigorous minority recruitment" and other race-neutral alternatives to the current policy would not yield a "sufficiently diverse student body."

Generally setting the bar for admission to the Michigan Law School was a "selection index" based on applicants' composite LSAT score and undergraduate GPA. A 1992 policy statement, however, made an explicit commitment to "racial and ethnic diversity," seeking to enroll a "critical mass" of black, Mexican-American, and Native American students. The objective was to enroll minority students in sufficient numbers to enable their participation in classroom discussions without feeling "isolated or like spokesmen for their race." To foster, "distinctive perspectives and experiences," admission officers consider a range of "soft variables"—e.g., talents, interests, experiences, and "underrepresented minority" status—in their admissions decisions. In the course of each year's admissions process, the record showed, minority admission rates were regularly reported to track "the racial composition of the developing class." The 1992 policy replaced an earlier "special admissions program," which set a written goal of 10-12% minority enrollment and lower academic requirements for those groups. The district court in *Grutter* made several key findings: there is a "heavy emphasis" on race in the law school admissions process; that over a period of time (1992-

1998) minorities ranged from 11% to17% of each incoming class; and that large numbers of minority students were admitted with index scores the same as or lower than unsuccessful white applicants.

Writing for the Sixth Circuit majority, Judge Martin adopted the Powell position in *Bakke* to find that the law school had a compelling interest in achieving a racially diverse student body, and that its admission's policy was "narrowly tailored" to that end. "Soft variables" were found to treat each applicant as an individual and to be "virtually indistinguishable" from "plus factors" and the Harvard Plan approved by Justice Powell in *Bakke*. The law school's policy "did not set-aside or reserve" seats on the basis of race. Rather, in pursuit of a "critical mass," the policy was designed to ensure that a "meaningful number" of minority students were able "to contribute to classroom dialogue without feeling isolated." The majority opinion further emphasized that the admissions program was "flexible," with no "fixed goal or target;" that it did not use "separate tracks" for minority and nonminority candidates; and did not function as a "quota system."

Without waiting for a final appeals court decision, the Supreme Court agreed to review the *Gratz* undergraduate admissions case in tandem with the Sixth Circuit ruling in *Grutter*. The Supreme Court handed down its rulings in *Grutter* and *Gratz* in 2003. Writing for the majority in the former was Justice O'Connor, who was joined by Justices Stevens, Souter, Ginsburg, and Breyer in upholding the Law School admissions policy. Chief Justice Rehnquist authored an opinion, in which Justices O'Connor, Scalia, Kennedy, and Thomas joined, striking down the University's undergraduate racial admissions program. Justice Breyer added a sixth vote to invalidate the racial bonus system in *Gratz*, but declined to join the majority opinion.

## The *Grutter* Decision

A notable aspect of the *Grutter* majority opinion was the degree to which it echoed the Powell rationale from *Bakke*. Settling, for the present, the doctrinal imbroglio that had consumed so much recent lower court attention, Justice O'Connor quoted extensively from Justice Powell's opinion, finding it to be the "touchstone for constitutional analysis of race-conscious admissions policies." But her opinion was not without its own possible doctrinal innovations. Overarching much of her reasoning were two paramount themes, that drew considerable criticism from Justice Thomas and his fellow dissenters. First, in applying "strict scrutiny" to the racial aspects of the Law School admissions program, Justice O'Connor stressed the situational nature of constitutional interpretation, taking "relevant differences into account." Thus, the majority opined, "[c]ontext matters when reviewing race-based governmental action" for equal protection purposes and "[n]ot every decision influenced by race is equally objectionable," but may depend upon "the importance and the sincerity of the reasons advanced by the governmental decisionmaker" for that particular use of race. Second, and equally significant, was the deference accorded to the judgment of educational decision-makers in defining the scope of their academic mission, even in regard to matters of racial and ethnic diversity. "[U]niversities occupy a special niche in our constitutional tradition," Justice O'Connor stated, such that "[t]he Law School's educational judgment ... that diversity is essential to its educational mission is one to which we defer." Institutional "good faith" would be "presumed" in the absence of contrary evidence. Justice Thomas's dissent, joined by Justice Scalia, took particular exception to what he viewed as "the fundamentally flawed proposition that racial discrimination can be contextualized"—deemed "compelling" for one purpose but not another—or that strict scrutiny permits "any sort of deference" to "the Law School's conclusion that its racial experimentation leads to educational benefits." Indeed, the dissenters found such deference to be "antithetical" to the level of searching review demanded by strict scrutiny.

Satisfied that the Law School had "compelling" reasons for pursuing a racially diverse student body, the Court moved to the second phase of strict scrutiny analysis. "Narrow tailoring," as noted, requires a close fit between "means" and "end" when the state draws any distinction based on race. In *Grutter*, the concept of "critical mass," so troubling to several Justices at oral argument, won the majority's approval as "necessary to further its compelling interest in securing the educational benefits of a diverse student body." In this portion of her opinion, Justice O'Connor drew chapter and verse from the standards articulated by Justice Powell in *Bakke*.

> We find that the Law School's admissions program bears the hallmarks of a narrowly tailored plan. As Justice Powell made clear in *Bakke*, truly individualized consideration demands that race be used in a flexible, nonmechanical way. It follows from this mandate that universities cannot establish quotas for members of certain racial groups or put members of those groups on separate admissions tracks. Nor can universities insulate applicants who belong to certain racial or ethnic groups from the competition for admission. Universities can, however, consider race or ethnicity more flexibly as a "plus" factor in the context of individualized consideration of each and every applicant.

Justice O'Connor drew a key distinction between forbidden "quotas" and permitted "goals," exonerating the Law School's admission program from constitutional jeopardy. She observed that both approaches pay "some attention to numbers." But while the former are "fixed" and "reserved exclusively for certain minority groups," the opinion continued, the Law School's "goal of attaining a critical mass" of minority students required only a "good faith effort" by the institution. In addition, Justice O'Connor noted, minority Law School enrollment between 1993 and 2000 varied from 13.5 to 20.1%, "a range inconsistent with a quota." Responding, in his separate dissent, the Chief Justice objected that the notion of a "critical mass" was a "sham," or subterfuge for "racial balancing," since it did not explain disparities in the proportion of the three minority groups admitted under its auspices.

Other factors further persuaded the Court that the Law School admissions process was narrowly tailored. By avoiding racial or ethnic "bonuses," the policy permitted consideration of "all pertinent elements of diversity," racial and nonracial, in "a highly individualized, holistic review of each applicant's file." Justice O'Connor also found that "race neutral alternatives" had been "sufficiently considered" by the Law School, although few specific examples are provided. Importantly, however, the opinion made plain that "exhaustion" of "every conceivable alternative" is not constitutionally required, only a "serious good faith consideration of workable race-neutral alternatives that will achieve the diversity the university seeks." Consequently, the Law School was not required to consider a lottery or lowering of traditional academic benchmarks—GPA and LSAT scores—for all applicants since "these alternatives would require a dramatic sacrifice of diversity, the academic quality of all admitted students, or both." And, because the admissions program was based on individual assessment of all pertinent elements of diversity, it did not "unduly burden" non-minority applicants. Nonetheless, as she had during oral argument, Justice O'Connor emphasized the need for "reasonable durational provisions," and "periodic reviews" by institutions conducting such programs. To drive home the point, the majority concludes with a general admonition. "We expect that 25 years from now, the use of racial preferences will no longer be necessary to further the interest approved today."

Besides Justices Thomas and Scalia, and the Chief Justice, another dissenting opinion was filed by Justice Kennedy, who agreed with his brethren that the "constancy" of minority admissions over a period of years "raised a suspicion" of racial balancing that the Law School was required by the rigors of strict scrutiny to rebut. Arguing from different statistics than the majority, he found "little deviation among admitted minority students from 1995 to 1998," which "fluctuated only by 0.3% from 13.5% to 13.8" and "at no point fell below 12%, historically defined by the Law School as the bottom of its critical mass range." In addition, he contended, the use of daily reports on minority admissions near the end of the process shifted the focus from individualized review of each applicant to institutional concerns for the numerical objective defined by a "critical mass." For these reasons, he agreed with his fellow dissenters that deference to the Law School in this situation was "antithetical to strict scrutiny, not consistent with it."

## The *Gratz* Decision

The four *Grutter* dissenters were joined by Justices O'Conner and Breyer in striking down the racial bonus system for undergraduate admissions in *Gratz*. Basically, the same factors that saved the Law School policy, by their absence, conspired to condemn the undergraduate program, in the eyes of the majority. Since the university's "compelling" interest in racial student diversity was settled in *Grutter*, the companion case focused on the reasons why the automatic award of 20 admission points to minority applicants failed the narrow tailoring aspect of strict scrutiny analysis. Relying, again, on the Powell rationale in *Bakke*, the policy was deemed more than a "plus" factor, as it denied each applicant "individualized consideration" by making race "decisive" for "virtually every minimally qualified underrepresented minority applicant." Nor did the procedure for "flagging" individual applications for additional review rescue the policy since "such consideration is the exception and not the rule," occurring—if at all—only after the "bulk of admission decisions" are made based on the point system. The opinion of the Chief Justice rejected the University's argument based on "administrative convenience," that the volume of freshman applications makes it "impractical" to apply a more individualized review. "[T]he fact that the implementation of a program capable of providing individualized consideration might present administrative challenges does not render constitutional an otherwise problematic system." Finally, the majority made plain that its constitutional holding in *Gratz* is fully applicable to private colleges and universities pursuant to the federal civil rights laws. "We have explained that discrimination that violates the Equal Protection Clause of the Fourteenth

Amendment committed by an institution that accepts federal funds also constitutes a violation of Title VI [of the 1964 Civil Rights Act]."

Justice O'Connor, concurring in *Gratz*, emphasized the "mechanical" and "automatic" nature of the selection index scoring, which distinguished it from the Law School program, and made impossible any "nuanced judgments" concerning "the particular background, experiences, or qualities of each particular candidate." She agreed that the Admissions Review Committee was "kind of an afterthought," particularly since the record was barren of evidence concerning its methods of operation and "how the decisions are actually made."

Dissenting opinions were filed jointly, by Justices Stevens and Souter, and separately by Justice Ginsburg. The former argued on technical grounds that since the named petitioners had already enrolled in other schools, and were not presently seeking freshman admission at the university, they lacked standing to seek prospective relief and the appeal should be dismissed. But Justice Souter argued separately on the merits that the Michigan undergraduate admission program was sufficiently different from the racial quota in *Bakke* to be constitutionally acceptable. At the very least, he felt, a more appropriate course would be to remand the case for further development of the record to determine whether the entire "admissions process, including review by the [Admissions Review Committee], results in individualized review sufficient to meet the Court's standards." Justice Ginsburg found "no constitutional infirmity" in the Michigan program since only "qualified" applicants are admitted, the current policy is not intended "to limit or decrease" admissions of any racial or ethnic group, and admissions of nonminority groups is not "unduly restricted." More broadly, she opined that government decision-makers may properly distinguish between policies of inclusion and exclusion, because the former are more likely to comport with constitutional imperatives of individual equality.

## Desegregation and Racial Diversity in Public Elementary, Secondary, and Magnet Schools (K-12)

The use of different cutoff scores for admission of white and minority students to magnet or other special schools within a public school system that formerly was illegally segregated has been the source of considerable controversy. In 1974, for example, courts found the Boston schools to be unlawfully segregated and ordered into effect a desegregation plan requiring, among other things, a thirty-five percent set-aside for admission of black and Hispanic students to the city's three "examination" schools.[38] This policy was revised to eliminate the set-aside after a successful equal protection challenge was brought in 1996 by a white student who was denied admission to the famed Boston Latin School.[39] Under the new policy, half of the available seats at each school was awarded solely on the basis of students' composite scores, derived from grade point averages and entrance examination scores. The other half was also awarded according to composite score rankings, but in conjunction with "flexible racial/ethnic guidelines." The guidelines required that these seats be allocated by composite rank score in proportion to the racial and ethnic composition of each school's remaining qualified applicant pool. A white student denied admission for the 1997-98 academic year, despite higher qualifications than several admitted minority students, challenged the guidelines on equal protection grounds.

In *Wessman v. Gittens*,[40] the First Circuit reversed a judgment in favor of the Boston School Committee, which had adopted the two-track admissions policy. The district court had applied strict scrutiny, but nonetheless concluded that the policy was constitutional based on the school system's compelling interests in diversity and in "overcoming the vestiges of past discrimination and avoiding the re-segregation of the Boston Public Schools." According to the appeals court, however, the School Committee had not produced sufficient evidence to demonstrate a compelling interest in either goal or that the admissions policy was narrowly tailored to those ends. First, there was no "solid and compelling evidence" that student diversity was "in any way tied to the vigorous exchange of ideas," nor that any achievement gap between minority and non-minority students amounted to "vestiges" of the system's past discrimination. The policy also swept "too broadly" by dividing individuals into "only five groups—blacks, whites, Hispanic, Asians, and Native Americans—without recognizing that none is monolithic." Thus, even assuming that diversity might, in some circumstances, be sufficiently compelling to justify race-conscious actions, "the School Committee's flexible racial/ethnic guidelines appear to be less a means of attaining diversity in any constitutionally relevant sense and more a means of racial balancing," which is neither "a legitimate [n]or necessary means of advancing the lofty principles credited in the policy."[41]

Meanwhile, in a pair of decisions, the Fourth Circuit invalidated affirmative action policies for admission of minority students to magnet schools in Arlington County, Va. and Montgomery County, Md. Because neither policy was found to satisfy the "narrow tailoring" aspect of strict scrutiny as required by *Adarand*, however, it was unnecessary for the court to decide whether educational diversity may be a "compelling interest" justifying race based admissions in other circumstances. At issue in the Arlington County case, *Tuttle v. Arlington County School Board*,[42] was a "sequential, weighted random lottery" system developed in response to prior litigation which took account of three factors—low-income background, the applicant's primary language, and race or ethnicity—in determining admission to three county magnet schools. The probabilities associated with each applicant's lottery number were weighted, so that members of under-represented groups, as defined by any of those factors, had an increased probability of selection. In the Montgomery County case, *Eisenberg v. Montgomery County Public Schools*,[43] school officials considered a variety of factors, including a "diversity profile" of affected schools, when deciding whether to grant applications for transfer from a student's assigned school to another county public school. The diversity profile, in effect, precluded transfer of students of a particular racial or ethnic background—white, black, Asian or Hispanic—from any school where the percentage of that group in the student body had declined over the preceding three years and was under-represented when compared to the county as a whole. In both cases, the challenged policy led to white students being denied admission to schools of their choice for racial reasons tied to student diversity.

While the Arlington County school system, earlier in its history, had been found to be *de jure* segregated and was required to desegregate by judicial decree, Montgomery County had never been subject to court supervised desegregation. Rather, the Maryland district had dismantled its formerly segregated schools by voluntary means, one aspect of which included implementation of a magnet school program. In neither case, however, did the Fourth Circuit attribute a remedial purpose to the diversity interest asserted by the school board, but found that the admissions and transfer policies in question were an exercise in "racial balancing." In so doing, the appeals court sidestepped deciding whether racial diversity in education could ever be a "compelling" state interest, proceeding instead to find the challenged policies failed the narrow tailoring aspect of *Adarand* analysis. In the Arlington case, the school board was found to have disregarded "one or more race-neutral policies" recommended by an advisory committee as alternatives to promote diversity. The duration of the plan was criticized for being "in perpetuity" and without "a logical stopping point." Although the weighted lottery did not "set-aside" positions for minorities, according to the court, the practical effect was the same since it "skew[ed] the odds of selection" in their favor to achieve classroom diversity "in proportions that approximate the distribution of students from [racial] groups in the district's overall student population." Finally, the plan lacked flexibility and impermissibly burdened "innocent third parties" who are denied admission for racial or ethnic reasons. Montgomery County's race-conscious transfer policy was characterized by the court as "mere racial balancing in a pure form" due to many of the same failings and because it was not directed at the correction of any past constitutional wrongs.

> The County annually ascertains the percentage of enrolled public school students by race on a county-wide basis, and then does the same for each school. It then assigns a numbered category for each race at each school, and administers the transfer policy so that the race and percentage in each school to which students are assigned by residence is compared to the percentage of that race in the countywide system. The transfer policy is administered with an object toward maintaining this percentage of racial balance in each school.... Although the transfer policy does not necessarily apply 'hard and fast quotas,' its goal of keeping certain percentages of racial/ethnic groups within each school to ensure diversity is racial balancing.[44]

Montgomery County officials were directed to eliminate the consideration of race from student transfer decisions, while in the Arlington case, further proceedings in the district court were ordered to review alternative admissions policies.

The U.S. Supreme Court in 2002 denied review of the Fourth Circuit *en banc* decision in *Belk v. Charlotte Mecklenburg Board of Education*.[45] The appeals court there affirmed a finding that "all vestiges of past discrimination" had been erased from the school system where student busing was first approved by the Supreme Court as a desegregation remedy. Because of its newly achieved "unitary status," the district court had relinquished jurisdiction of the desegregation case and ordered the school district to stop "assigning children to schools or allocating educational opportunities and benefits through race-based lotteries, preferences, set-asides or other means that deny students an equal footing based on race." The specific target of the judge's order was the "race-conscious policy for admission of students to the magnet school program operated by the district for desegregation purposes."[46]

A majority of the *en banc* appellate court affirmed that the school district had eliminated the "last vestiges" of unconstitutional segregation to the fullest extent "practicable." Any remaining racial concentrations, therefore, were a consequence of factors—namely residential segregation— beyond the power of school authorities or the courts to control. In a unitary setting, the magnet admissions process could not clear the first hurdle by showing a compelling governmental interest, and the school district could not make "any further use of race-based lotteries, preferences, and set-asides in student assignment." A slightly different majority ruled that the school board could not be held liable for its use of race in assigning students to magnet schools since the program had originated in a then valid desegregation order. But if the same plan were adopted after the district is declared unitary, it would clearly be unconstitutional under *Tuttle* and *Eisenberg*, these judges opined.

The issue before the Fourth Circuit in *Belk* focused on whether the school board, in creating its admission plan, was acting beyond what was permitted to comply with the court's desegregation order. Another ruling, by the Fifth Circuit, in *Cavalier v. Caddo Parish School Board*,[47] also suggests that educational authorities have broader discretion to consider race in making admissions decisions when the school district is under a court order to desegregate. *Cavalier* held that a magnet school preferential admissions program that mandated a 50% to 50% (plus or minus 15%) racial student mix, and imposed lower minimum standardized test scores for minority than white applicants, was not narrowly tailored to a compelling governmental interest. The school board relied exclusively on a 1981 consent decree ordering desegregation to prove a compelling governmental interest. Magnet schools had been released from the decree in 1990, however. And the appeals court found that while student body diversity provided compelling justification for considering race in law school admissions under *Grutter*, "it is by no means clear that it could be such at or below the high school level."[48] The admission plan was additionally flawed for its failure to consider race-neutral means to achieve student body diversity and was a quota system. Student selections were made from two separate lists of applicant students, one for black student and one for white students, without direct comparison of candidates to the applicant pool at large. Insulating students of one racial group from competition with the larger admissions pool, along with the 50% goal, amounted to an impermissible quota.

The diversity issue has also arisen in another educational setting. The University of California operates a popular elementary school as a "laboratory" to research urban education and "to foster a more effective educational system primarily for urban elementary students." Beyond basic research, the school develops new techniques for educating students in multicultural urban settings and conducts seminars, workshops, and teacher training programs throughout the state. The school considers applicants' race and ethnicity to obtain adequate cross-samples of the general population and thus to maintain "the scientific credibility of its educational studies." The plaintiff in *Hunter v. Regents of the University of California*[49] challenged the school's admissions policy as an equal protection violation. While perhaps not tantamount to a diversity rationale, the Ninth Circuit nonetheless agreed with the district court judge that the state's interest in "operating a research-oriented elementary school dedicated to improving the quality of education in urban public schools" was compelling even absent any purpose of remedying past discrimination.

> The challenges posed by California's increasingly diverse population intensify the state's interest in improving urban public schools. Cultural and economic differences in the classroom pose special difficulties for public school teachers. In his decision, Judge Kenyon noted that defendants presented 'an exhaustive list of such issues and challenges [that] includes limited language proficiency, different learning styles, involvement of parents from diverse cultures with different expectations and values, and racial and ethnic conflict among families and children.' [An expert witness] stated that '[t]here is no more pressing problem, facing California, or indeed the nation, than urban education; for it is in the urban school system that the majority of California's future citizens will be educated (either well or poorly), creating the basic fabric for the society of the future.' ... Given this record, the district court concluded, and we agree, that 'the defendants' interest in operating a research-oriented elementary school is compelling.'[50]

Given the demographics of California's urban population, and the necessity of creating a multicultural laboratory setting, the consideration of race for admission to the school was deemed "narrowly tailored" since "it would not be possible, nor would it be reasonable, to require defendants to attempt to obtain an ethnically diverse representative sample of students without specific racial target and classifications."[51]

Meanwhile, although the Supreme Court in *Grutter* did not address the voluntary use of race as a factor in achieving diversity in elementary and secondary education, all three appeals courts to consider the issue after *Grutter* and *Gratz* were decided upheld racial diversity measures in public schools.[52] In *Comfort v. Lynn School Committee*,[53] the U.S. Court of Appeals for the First Circuit issued an *en banc* decision holding that a school district use of race as a factor in its student assignment plan does not violate the Equal Protection Clause. Relying on principles laid down by *Grutter* and *Gratz*, the First Circuit concluded that the plan's goal of securing the educational benefits of racial diversity constituted a compelling interest and that the plan was narrowly tailored to achieve that goal. The ruling reversed an earlier three-judge appellate panel's contrary conclusion that the consideration of race in Lynn's voluntary school choice plan was unconstitutional.

Under Massachusetts's Racial Imbalance Act, local communities received additional state education aid if they adopted plans that assigned students on the basis of race. The City of Lynn School Committee implemented a voluntary desegregation plan that allowed all students to attend neighborhood schools. Race only became a factor when a student sought to transfer to another school. The transfer was permitted only if it would not increase the racial imbalance at either the sending or receiving school. Citizens for the Preservation of Constitutional Rights (CPCR) filed suit on behalf of several parents. A federal district court ruled that the plan satisfied equal protection requirements. On appeal, the three-judge panel reversed the district court, ruling that while the goal of student body diversity constituted a compelling state interest, the plan was not narrowly tailored to that end.

The panel decision was withdrawn when the First Circuit granted Lynn's motion for a rehearing *en banc*. Addressing the "compelling state interest" prong of the equal protection test, the full court measured the plan against the law school admissions policy upheld in *Grutter*. The court rejected CPCR's assertion that *Grutter's* recognition of a compelling interest in

> 'the educational benefits that flow from student body diversity' ... is ... limited to the benefits that flow from viewpoint diversity in the higher education context and does not extend to the benefits that flow from racial diversity in the K-12 context.

The First Circuit, however, found that the educational benefits found compelling in *Grutter* were advanced not only by viewpoint diversity, but also by racial diversity, and these interests were no less strong in K-12 than in higher education.

Turning to the "narrowly tailored " prong, the court noted that while the Supreme Court had yet to consider the question, *Grutter* and *Gratz* provided sufficient guidance to determine the constitutionality of a voluntary K-12 race-based assignment policy. Because the Lynn plan dealt with a noncompetitive transfer policy, as opposed to competitive admissions policies, competition-related criteria—such as need for individualized consideration of applicants, so important in *Grutter/Gratz*—were not relevant here. Otherwise, the court found that the plan's use of race was minimally invasive; avoided racial balancing for its own sake; avoided use of quotas; was of finite duration; and was adopted after considering race-neutral alternatives.

In *MacFarland v. Jefferson County Public Schools*,[54] issued on the first anniversary of the Michigan decisions and the 50th anniversary of *Brown v. Board of Education*, a federal district court in Kentucky upheld a Louisville district's voluntary consideration of race in making student assignments to achieve racial integration in the public schools. Jefferson County Public Schools (JCPS) were ordered by judicial decree to desegregate in 1975. Under the desegregation plan, each school was to have between 15% and 50% African-American enrollment and students were bused, if necessary, to ensure racial diversity. Twenty-five years later, in 2000, the federal courts ended their supervision of the desegregation plan, but the JCPS voluntarily opted to maintain its integrated schools through a "managed choice" plan. The plan was challenged in a lawsuit by black parents whose children were denied admission to Central High School, which was already at the upper percentage limit for minority enrollment.

The district court found that the managed choice plan served numerous compelling state interests, "some of the same reasons for integrated schools that the Supreme Court upheld in *Grutter*." Thus, Judge Heyburn accepted the school board's arguments that the plan improved the educational experience; that it produced educational benefits for students of all races over the last 25 years; and that it helped overcome the adverse effects of concentrations of poverty that impact black students to a greater extent than whites. "Integrated schools, better academic performance, appreciation for our diverse heritage and stronger, more competitive public schools are consistent with the central values and themes of American culture," Judge Heyburn wrote. The court also found that the student assignment plan was "narrowly tailored" in every respect except for its use of separate "racial categories," which the district was required to revise for the 2005-2006 school year. For reasons "articulated in the well-reasoned opinion of the district court," the Sixth Circuit summarily affirmed Judge Heyburn's decree, without issuing a detailed written opinion.[55]

The constitutionality of race-conscious admissions to magnet or alternative schools, designed to promote elementary and secondary school desegregation, has also been before the courts. In *Parents Involved in Community Schools v. Seattle School District No. 1*,[56] the Ninth Circuit applied *Grutter* and *Gratz* to approve a school district's plan to maintain racially diverse schools. Under Seattle's "controlled choice" high school student assignment plan, students were given the option to attend high schools across the district, but if the demand for seats exceeded the supply at a particular school, a student's race was considered as a tie-breaker in determining admittance to the oversubscribed school. The racial tie-breaker applied only to schools whose student bodies deviated by more than 15 percentage points from the overall racial makeup of the district, then "approximately 40% white and 60% nonwhite." The Seattle plan was voluntarily adopted to "achiev[e] diversity [and] limit racial isolation" in the schools, not as a part of a desegregation remedy.

In an *en banc* decision, the Ninth Circuit ruled that the school district had a compelling interest in the educational and social benefits of racial diversity and in avoiding racially concentrated or isolated schools. Further, the court held that the district's plan was sufficiently narrowly tailored to pass constitutional muster. According to the court, the "individualized" and "holistic" review endorsed by the Supreme Court was not required of a noncom-petitive, voluntary student assignment plan such as Seattle's, as long as the plan was otherwise narrowly tailored. The court held that Seattle's plan was sufficiently narrowly tailored, concluding that the 15 percentage point "band" was not a quota because it was flexible and did not reserve a certain number of fixed slots based on race. The court also ruled that the school district had made a good faith effort to consider race-neutral alternatives. Finally, the court concluded that the plan imposed a minimal burden—not being permitted to attend one's preferred school—that was shared by all students and that the plan, which was subject to regular reviews, was sufficiently limited in time and in scope. The ruling reversed an earlier three-judge appellate panel's contrary decision that the school district's plan to maintain racially diverse schools was not sufficiently narrowly tailored.

As noted above, the Supreme Court had never, until recently, considered the constitutionality of the voluntary use of race as a factor in achieving diversity in elementary and secondary education. All three of the federal appeals courts to consider the issue since *Grutter* and *Gratz* were decided upheld racial diversity measures in public schools,[57] but these opinions conflicted with pre*Grutter*/*Gratz* appellate rulings that rejected such racially based plans.[58] Possibly as a result of this conflict, the Supreme Court granted review in *MacFarland v. Jefferson County Public Schools*—now *Meredith v. Jefferson County Board of Education*—and *Parents Involved in Community Schools v. Seattle School District No. 1* to consider the question of what steps, if any, a public school district may take to maintain racial diversity in elementary and secondary education.[59]

In *Parents Involved in Community Schools v. Seattle School District No. 1*, a consolidated ruling that resolved both cases, the Court ultimately struck down the school plans at issue, holding that they violated the equal protection guarantee of the Fourteenth Amendment.[60]

## The *Parents Involved in Community Schools* Decision

Ultimately, the Supreme Court held that the Louisville and Seattle school plans violated the equal protection clause. However, the decision was fractured, with five different Justices filing opinions in the case. Announcing the judgment of the Court was Chief Justice Roberts, who led a plurality of four Justices in concluding that the school plans were unconstitutional because they did not serve a compelling governmental interest. Although Justice Kennedy, who concurred in the Court's judgment striking down the plans, disagreed with the plurality's conclusion that the diversity plans did not serve a compelling governmental interest, he found that the school plans were unconstitutional because they were not narrowly tailored. In addition, Justice Thomas filed a concurring opinion, and Justices Stevens and Breyer filed separate dissenting opinions.

In the portion of his opinion that was joined by Justice Kennedy and that therefore announced the judgment of the Court, Chief Justice Roberts began by noting that the Court had jurisdiction in the case, thereby rejecting a challenge to the standing of the plaintiff organization Parents Involved in Community Schools (PICS).[61] Chief Justice Roberts then turned to the substantive merits of the claims involved, reiterating that governmental racial classifications must be reviewed under strict scrutiny. As a result, the Court examined whether the school districts had demonstrated that their assignment and transfer plans were narrowly tailored to achieve a compelling governmental interest.

In assessing the compelling interest prong of the strict scrutiny test, Chief Justice Roberts noted that the Court has recognized two interests that qualify as compelling where the use of racial classifications in the school context is concerned: remedying the effects of past intentional discrimination and promoting diversity in higher education. However, the Chief Justice found that neither of these interests was advanced by the school plans at issue. According to the Chief Justice, because Seattle schools were never intentionally segregated and because the lifting of its desegregation order demonstrated that Louisville schools had successfully remediated past discrimination in its schools, neither school district could assert a compelling interest in remedying past intentional discrimination.[62]

Likewise, the Court argued that the *Grutter* precedent did not govern the current cases. According to Chief Justice Roberts, the compelling interest recognized in *Grutter* was in a broadly defined diversity that encompassed more than just racial diversity and that focused on each applicant as an individual. Because race was the only factor considered by the school districts rather than other factors that reflected a broader spectrum of diverse qualifications and characteristics and because the plans did not provide individualized review of applicants, the plurality opinion found that the school districts' articulated interest in diversity was not compelling. Added the Chief Justice, "[e]ven when it comes to race, the plans here employ only a limited notion of diversity, viewing race exclusively in white/nonwhite terms in Seattle and black/'other' terms in Jefferson County."[63] In rejecting *Grutter* as applicable precedent, the Court also noted that the decision had rested in part on the unique considerations of higher education and that those considerations were absent in the elementary and secondary education context.

Even if the school districts had met the first prong of the strict scrutiny test by establishing a compelling governmental interest in the use of racial classifications to make school assignments, the Court found the school plans would still have failed the second prong of the test because they were not sufficiently narrowly tailored to meet their stated goals. According to Chief Justice Roberts, in both Seattle and Louisville, only a few students were assigned to a non-preferred school based on race. As a result, "the minimal impact of the districts' racial classifications on school enrollment casts doubt on the necessity of using racial classifications,"[64] especially in light of the fact that such racial classifications are permissible in only the most extreme circumstances. Additionally, the Court was concerned that the school districts had failed to consider methods other than racial classifications to achieve their goals, despite a requirement that narrowly tailored programs consider race-neutral alternatives.

Although Justice Kennedy joined the above portions of the plurality opinion, thereby forming a majority in favor of striking down the school plans, he did not join the remainder of the plurality opinion, which concluded for additional reasons that the school plans were unconstitutional. In these portions of his opinion, Chief Justice Roberts faulted the school plans for tying their diversity goals to each district's specific racial demographics rather than to "any pedagogical concept of the level of diversity needed to obtain the asserted educational benefits."[65] In other words, each district tried to establish schools with racial diversity that mirrored the percentages of racial groups in their respective overall populations. This effort, according to the Chief Justice, amounted to unconstitutional racial balancing because the plans were not in fact narrowly tailored to the goal of achieving the educational and social benefits that allegedly flow from racial diversity but rather were tailored to racial demographics instead. Indeed, Chief Justice Roberts wrote, "[a]ccepting racial balancing as a compelling state interest would justify the imposition of racial proportionality throughout American society, contrary to our repeated recognition that at the heart of the Constitution's guarantee of equal protection lies the simple command that the Government must treat citizens as individuals, not as simply components of a racial, religious, sexual or national class."[66] Such racial balancing could not, in the Chief Justice's view, amount to a compelling governmental interest even if pursued in the name of racial diversity or racial integration.

In another portion of the plurality opinion not joined by Justice Kennedy, Chief Justice Roberts criticized Justice Breyer's dissent for misapplying precedents that recognized a compelling interest in remedying past discrimination. According to the Chief Justice, the Court has recognized a compelling interest in remedying past discrimination when that discrimination is caused by governmental action but not when caused by other factors, such as social or economic pressures. Noting that the Seattle school district was never segregated due to state action and the Louisville school district had eliminated all vestiges of state segregation, the Chief Justice therefore argued that the cases cited by Justice Breyer as precedents for race-conscious school integration efforts were inapplicable to the current case.[67] The plurality opinion concluded with a discussion of *Brown v. Board of Education*,[68] in which the Court held that the deliberate segregation of schoolchildren by race was unconstitutional. According to the plurality:

> Before *Brown*, schoolchildren were told where they could and could not go to school based on the color of their skin. The school districts in these cases have not carried the heavy burden of demonstrating that we should allow this once again—even for very different reasons.... The way to stop discrimination on the basis of race is to stop discriminating on the basis of race.[69]

Although he joined the Court in striking down the school plans, Justice Kennedy wrote a separate concurring opinion that provides additional insight into how the Justices might handle future cases involving the consideration of race in the educational context. As noted above, Justice Kennedy declined to sign on to the plurality opinion in full, in part because he disagreed with its implication that diversity in elementary and secondary education, at least as properly defined, does not serve a compelling governmental interest. According to Justice Kennedy, "[d]iversity, depending on its meaning and definition, is a compelling educational goal a school district may pursue,"[70] but neither Seattle nor Louisville had shown that its plans served a compelling interest in promoting diversity or that the plans were narrowly tailored to achieve that goal.

Justice Kennedy also pointedly criticized the plurality opinion for "imply[ing] an all-toounyielding insistence that race cannot be a factor in instances when, in my view, it may be taken into account. ...In the administration of public schools by the state and local authorities, it is permissible to consider the racial makeup of schools and to adopt general policies to encourage a diverse student body, one aspect of which is its racial composition."[71] Justice Kennedy identified several ways in which schools, in his view, could constitutionally pursue racial diversity or avoid racial isolation, including strategic site selection of new schools, altering attendance zones, providing resources for special programs, and recruiting students and faculty. According to Justice Kennedy, such measures would be constitutional because, while race-conscious, they are not based on classifications that treat individuals differently based on race. However, Justice Kennedy would not limit schools to facially neutral methods of achieving diversity, saying that racial classifications might be permissible if based on "a more nuanced, individual evaluation of school needs and student characteristics" similar to the plan approved in *Grutter*.[72] Although no other justice joined his concurrence, Justice Kennedy's unique role in providing the pivotal swing vote in the case makes his concurring opinion significant to any future legal developments regarding the use of racial classifications in the education context.

Although Justice Thomas joined the plurality opinion written by Chief Justice Roberts in full, he also wrote a separate concurring opinion that took issue with certain aspects of Justice Breyer's dissent. Among other things, Justice Thomas disagreed with the dissent's assertion that the school plans were necessary to combat school resegregation, arguing that neither Seattle nor Louisville faced the type of intentional state action to separate the races that the school districts in *Brown* had.[73] In addition, Justice Thomas contested the dissent's argument that a less strict standard of review should apply when racial classifications are used for benign purposes, in part because Justice Thomas disagreed that the school plans—which, he wrote, inevitably exclude some individuals based on race and therefore may exacerbate racial tension—are as benign as the dissent asserted. More importantly, Justice Thomas argued that the perception of what constitutes a benign use of race-conscious measures is nothing more than a reflection of current social practice that relies too heavily on the good intentions of current public officials. According to Justice Thomas, "if our history has taught us anything, it has taught us to beware of elites bearing racial theories," adding in a footnote, "Justice Breyer's good intentions, which I do not doubt, have the shelf life of Justice Breyer's tenure."[74]

As noted above, both Justices Stevens and Breyer dissented from the Court's decision to strike down the school plans. In his brief dissent, Justice Stevens, who also joined Justice Breyer's dissent, described the Court's reliance on *Brown* as a "cruel irony" because it ignored the historical context in which *Brown* was decided and the ways in which subsequent precedents applied the landmark decision to uphold school integration efforts.[75] Meanwhile, in a lengthy and passionate dissent nearly twice as long as Chief Justice Roberts's opinion, Justice Breyer argued that the Court's holding "distorts precedent, ... misapplies the relevant constitutional principles, ... announces legal rules that will obstruct efforts by state and local governments to deal effectively with the growing resegregation of public schools, ... threatens to substitute for present calm a disruptive round of race-related litigation, and ... undermines *Brown's* promise of integrated primary and secondary education that local communities have sought to make a reality."[76]

## Faculty Diversity

Corollary issues concerning faculty diversity have also been before the courts, including the *Piscataway* case, which was dismissed as moot by the Supreme Court after the parties reached an out-of-court settlement. The appeal from *Taxman v. Board of Education of Piscataway Township*[77] had asked the High Court to consider whether a local school board's desire to promote faculty diversity could legally justify its decision to protect a black teacher from layoff, while dismissing an equally qualified white colleague, in the absence of a showing of past discrimination or a "manifest" racial imbalance in its workforce. Two teachers, one white, the other black, were hired on the same day in 1980 and were deemed equally qualified for their positions in the business education department when a reduction in force became necessary eight years later. Minority teachers were not underrepresented on the overall faculty—constituting 9.5 % of the district's teachers versus 5.8 % of the relevant county labor pool—and no evidence of past discrimination by the school district was presented at trial. A "coin toss" had traditionally been used to determine retention rights among similarly situated employees in the past. But because only one black teacher was among the business department's ten-member staff, the school district relied on its affirmative action policy to retain the minority employee rather than her white colleague in the interests of promoting racial diversity.

An *en banc* majority of the Third Circuit determined that however laudable the school board's objective might be, laying off a white reacher "solely" on the basis of race to achieve faculty diversity exceeded the bounds of controlling Supreme Court precedent. Title VII rulings in *Weber* and *Johnson* permitted employers to make employment decisions based on race or gender in order to redress a "manifest" imbalance of minorities and women in "traditionally segregated job categories." But judicial teachings generally caution against affirmative action measures that "unnecessarily trammel" or frustrate the "legitimate and firmly rooted expectation in continued employment" of affected non-minorities. In its 1986 *Wygant* decision, the Court voided race-based layoff protection for minority public school teachers because of its immediate adverse impact on "identifiable" senior white employees. Consequently, while applauding the board's commitment to racial diversity, the *Taxman* appellate opinion rejected the non-remedial educational purposes asserted by the board for its affirmative action plan because "there is no congressional recognition of diversity as a Title VII objective requiring accommodation." And because the entire burden of the board's plan fell upon the white teacher whose interests were "unnecessarily trammeled" by the loss of her job, the race-based policy violated Title VII.

In 1998, the Supreme Court declined to review the legality of a "minority bonus policy" in an affirmative action plan established for Nevada's public colleges to redress a lack of minority faculty members. In *Farmer v. University and Community College Systems of Nevada,*[78] the plaintiff had been one of three finalists for a faculty position in the sociology department that the university awarded to a black male candidate from Uganda with "comparable" qualifications. The university's minority bonus policy, which the Nevada Supreme Court described as an "unwritten amendment" to its affirmative action plan, allowed a department to hire an additional faculty member following the initial placement of a minority candidate. As a consequence, the plaintiff was hired by the sociology department a year later, but at a lesser salary than the earlier-hired black candidate. The differential was defended by the university as reflecting a pay premium necessary "to prevent[ ] a bidding war between two prestigious universities slated to interview [the black candidate]." Farmer challenged both the hiring and pay decisions by the university as race and sex discrimination prohibited by Title VII and the Equal Pay Act.

The state supreme court reversed a jury verdict for the plaintiff and upheld the university's affirmative action hiring policy on both federal constitutional and statutory grounds. First, according to the court, race was only one factor considered by the university—along with educational background, publishing, teaching experience, etc.—in evaluating applicants. In contrast to *Piscataway*, the university faculty was a "white enclave" with only 1 % black members, a factor persuading the court that the university had a "compelling interest in fostering a culturally and ethnically diverse faculty" under standards laid out by the *Bakke* and *Weber* cases.

> Here, in addition to considerations of race, the University based its employment decision on such criteria as educational background, publishing, teaching experience, and areas of specialization. This satisfies *Bakke's* commands that race must be only one of several factors used in evaluating applicants. We also view the desirability of a racially diverse faculty as sufficiently analogous to the constitutionally permissible attainment of a racially diverse student body countenanced by the *Bakke* Court.

Thus, severe minority underrepresentation on the university faculty combined with the employer's consideration of relative qualifications in addition to race distinguished *Piscataway*, the Nevada court felt, and conformed the case to Justice Powell's *Bakke* opinion. In addition, the impact of the initial minority hire was mitigated by affording the disappointed white applicant a subsequent position created pursuant to informal practice or custom under the affirmative action policy.

## CONCLUSION

The Michigan cases resolved an issue that had vexed the lower federal courts for a quarter-century. Historically, judicial insistence on strict scrutiny has largely condemned governmental distinctions based on race, except in the most narrowly circumscribed remedial or national security circumstances. To the short list of governmental interests sufficiently "compelling" to warrant race-based decision-making, a majority of the Court added the pursuit of diversity in higher education. But this expansion has been curtailed somewhat by the Court's more recent pronouncement involving elementary and secondary school plans to promote racial diversity.

Although the Court's decision to strike down the Seattle and Louisville school assignment and transfer plans will have a profound impact on similar plans at many of the nation's elementary and secondary schools, the *Parents Involved in Community Schools* case did not completely foreclose the possibility that school districts may constitutionally pursue certain measures to avoid racial isolation, prevent resegregation, and promote racial diversity in their schools. However, it is not entirely clear what these measures might entail. While the facially race-neutral methods identified in Justice Kennedy's concurring opinion—such as engaging in strategic site selection of new schools, altering attendance zones, providing resources for special programs, and recruiting students and faculty—seem more likely to survive judicial scrutiny, the fate of other kinds of race-conscious school plans may become apparent only as a result of legal developments that emerge over time. Indeed, there is evidence that some school districts are abandoning race-based school assignment plans in favor of plans based on socioeconomic status, which is a non-suspect classification for purposes of constitutional review.[79]

Meanwhile, the seeds of future controversy may lie in questions arguably raised but not fully addressed by the latest rulings. For example, the Court's latest rulings left unanswered the constitutional status of racially exclusive diversity policies not directly involving admissions, such as the legality of race-based scholarship and financial aid, recruitment and outreach, or college preparation courses that exclusively target minority populations. In addition, the question of whether schools or universities may completely avoid constitutional shoals by adopting "race-neutral" plans to increase racial diversity may not be fully answered by the Court's latest rulings. Such race-neutral alternatives include "percentage plans" like those approved in Texas, Florida, and California that guarantee college admission to top graduates from every state high school, regardless of race. In addition to percentage plans, educational authorities have experimented with other forms of "alternative action," or policies designed to promote racial diversity without relying on racial preferences. "Class-based" affirmative action, for example, takes socioeconomic status or the family educational background of students into account. Florida has replaced race and ethnicity with other socio-economic and geographical proxies for diversity; increased the state's need-based financial aid program; sought to improve the state's lowest-performing primary and secondary schools; and provided free SAT prep courses at those schools. California state schools have targeted financial aid programs toward underprivileged neighborhoods as a means of reaching minority students. Another approach considers "diversity" or "hardship" essays in which applicants describe challenging life experiences such as poverty, English as a second language, or having a family member in prison. Some reformers advocate targeting additional resources to underperforming elementary and secondary schools as a way to address the root causes of minority underrepresentation in higher education.

By avoiding the use of explicit racial classifications and dual track admission policies, these efforts are far less susceptible to facial challenge as an equal protection violation. Programs involving the explicit consideration of race remain most at risk. But policies that employ nonracial factors as a proxy for race may be vulnerable if the purpose or intent is to benefit minority groups. In *Washington v. Davis*[80] and related rulings,[81] the Supreme Court determined that a race-neutral law with a disparate racial impact on minority groups is subject to strict scrutiny if it is enacted with a racially discriminatory purpose. Racial motive was made a constitutional "touchstone" for equal protection analysis, and whether reflected by a racial classification or other evidence of discriminatory purpose, strict scrutiny was triggered by evidence of such intent. Similarly, alternatives to traditional racial diversity policies may not escape strict judicial scrutiny if an objecting non-minority applicant is able to show that the plan was racially motivated. The same limitations may apply to private institutions, which are immune from constitutional limitations, under Title VI of the 1964 Civil Rights Act.

Beyond education, issues may inevitably arise concerning the implications of *Grutter* and *Parents Involved in Community Schools* on efforts to achieve racial diversity in other social and economic spheres. To date, the Court has permitted race-conscious hiring criteria by private employers under Title VII, either as a remedy for past discrimination or to redress a "conspicuous racial imbalance in traditionally segregated job categories,"[82] but refused to find that a state's interest in faculty diversity to provide teacher "role models" was sufficiently compelling to warrant a race-conscious layoff policy.[83] Lower courts are similarly divided, though a few have applied an "operational need analysis" to uphold police force diversity policies, recognizing "that 'a law enforcement body's need to carry out its mission effectively, with a workforce that appears unbiased, is able to communicate with the public and is respected by the community it serves,' may constitute a compelling state interest."[84] But current standards under the federal civil rights laws generally allow for consideration of race in hiring and promotion decisions only in response to demonstrable evidence of past discrimination by the employer or within the affected industry. No rule of deference like that extended to educational institutions has been recognized for employers, nor is one likely to be applied in the wake of *Parents Involved in Community Schools*.

## End Notes

[1] 438 U.S. 265 (1978).

[2] 78 F.3d 932, 944 (5th Cir. 1996) ("Justice Powell's view in *Bakke* is not binding precedent on the issue."), cert. denied, 518 U.S. 1033 (1996). See also Lutheran Church-Missouri Synod v. FCC, 141 F.3d 344, 354 (D.C.Cir. 1998) (stating, without addressing *Bakke*, that diversity cannot "be elevated to the 'compelling' level").

[3] See Brewer v. West Irondequoit Center School District, 212 F.3d 738, 747-49 (2d Cir. 2000) (noting that "there is much disagreement among the circuit courts as to ... the state of the law under current Supreme Court jurisprudence," but concluding that, regardless of *Bakke*, reducing racial isolation may be a compelling interest under Second Circuit precedent); Eisenberg v. Montgomery County Public Schools, 197 F.3d 123, 130 (4th Cir. 1999) (explaining that the status of educational diversity as a compelling interest is "unresolved," and rather than rule on the issue, decided the case solely on narrow tailoring grounds); Wessmann v. Gittens, 160 F.3d 790, 795, 800 (lst Cir. 1998) (While "[t]he question of precisely what interests government may legitimately invoke to justify race-based classifications is largely unsettled," the court concluded defendant's apparent interest in "racial balancing" of the student body was neither "a legitimate [n]or necessary means of advancing" diversity); Buchwald v. University of New Mexico School of Medicine, 159 F.3d 487, 499 (10th Cir. 1998) (noting the absence of "a clear majority opinion" in *Bakke*, but according qualified immunity to defendants who relied upon that case in adopting a preference based on durational residency); McNamara v. City of Chicago, 138 F.3d 1219, 1222 (7th Cir. 1998) (citing *Bakke* for statement that "whether there may be compelling interests other than remedying past discrimination remains 'unsettled,'" but finding defendant's remedial justification valid).

[4] Smith v. University of Washington Law School, 233 F.3d 1188, 1201 (9th Cir. 2000) (pursuant to *Bakke*, "educational diversity is a compelling governmental interest that meets the demands of strict scrutiny of race conscious measures"), cert. denied, 532 U.S. 1051 (2001).

[5] Gratz v. Bollinger, 122 F.Supp.2d 811 (E.D.Mich. 2000).

[6] Grutter v. Bollinger, 137 F. Supp. 2d 821, 848 (E.D. Mich. 2001) (concluding that "*Bakke* does not stand for the proposition that a university's desire to assemble a racially diverse student body is a compelling state interest").

[7] 539 U.S. 306 (2003).

[8] 539 U.S. 244 (2003).

[9] 416 F.3d 513 (6th Cir. 2003) (per curiam), cert. granted, 547 U.S. 1177 (2006); 426 F.3d 1162 (9th Cir. 2005) (en banc), cert. granted, 547 U.S. 1177 (2006).

[10] 127 S. Ct. 2738 (2007).

[11] See e.g. Green v. County Board, 391 U.S. 430 (1968); Swann v. Board of Education, 402 U.S. 1 (1971); Keyes v. Denver School District, 413 U.S. 189 (1973).

[12] Dowell v. Board of Education, 498 U.S. 237 (1991). See also Freeman v. Pitts, 503 U.S. 467 (1993) (allowing incremental dissolution of judicial control) and Missouri v. Jenkins, 515 U.S. 70 (1995) (directing district court on remand to "bear in mind that its end purpose is not only 'to remedy the violation' to the extent practicable, but also `to restore state and local authorities to the control of a school system that is operating in compliance with the Constitution.'").

[13] 42 U.S.C. 2000e-5(g).

[14] 29 C.F.R. Part 1608 (the guidelines state the EEOC's position that when employers voluntarily undertake in good faith to remedy past discrimination by race- or gender-conscious affirmative action means, the agency will not find them liable for reverse discrimination.).

[15] 42 U.S.C. 2000d et seq.

[16] 44 Fed. Reg. 58,509 (October 10, 1979).

[17] 59 Fed. Reg. 8756 (February 23, 1994). See also Letter from Judith A. Winston, General Counsel, United States Department of Education, to College and University Counsel, July 30, 1996 (reaffirming that it is permissible in appropriate circumstances for colleges and universities to consider race in admissions decisions and granting financial aid).

[18] Regents of Univ. of Cal. v. Bakke, 438 U.S. 265, 311-12 (1978).

[19] Id. at 317.

[20] 476 U.S. 267 (1986).

[21] Fullilove v. Klutznick, 448 U.S. 448 (1980).

[22] Metro Broadcasting, Inc. v. FCC, 497 U.S. 547 (1990).

[23] City of Richmond v. J.A. Croson Co., 488 U.S. 469 (1989).

[24] 42 U.S.C. §§ 2000e et seq.

[25] United Steelworkers v. Weber, 443 U.S. 193 (1979).

[26] Local 28 Sheet Metal Workers v. EEOC, 478 U.S. 421 (1986).

[27] United States v. Paradise, 480 U.S. 149 (1987); Johnson v. Transportation Agency, 480 U.S. 616 (1987).

[28] 488 U.S. 469 (1989).

[29] 497 U.S. 547 (1990).

[30] 515 U.S. 200 (1995).

[31] Regents of Univ. of Cal. v. Bakke, 438 U.S. 265, 315 (1978).

[32] 78 F.3d 932 (5th Cir. 1996), cert. denied 518 U.S. 1033 (1996).

[33] 263 F.3d 1234 (11th Cir. 2001).

[34] 233 F.3d 1188 (9th Cir. 2000).

[35] 430 U.S. 188 (1977).

[36] Gratz v. Bollinger, 122 F. Supp. 811 (E.D. Mich. 2000).

[37] Grutter v. Bollinger, 288 F.3d 732 (6th Cir. 2002).

[38] See Morgan v. Hennigan, 379 F. Supp. 410 (D. Mass), aff'd sub nom. Morgan v. Kerrigan, 509 F.2d 580 (lst Cir. 1974).

[39] See McLaughlin v. Boston School Committee, 938 F. Supp. 1001 (D.Mass. 1996).

[40] 160 F.3d 790 (lst Cir. 1998).

[41] Id. at 799.

[42] 195 F.3d 698 (4th Cir. 1999), cert. denied 529 U.S. 1050 (2000).

[43] 197 F.3d 123 (4th Cir. 1999), cert. denied 529 U.S. 1019 (2000).

[44] Id. at 133.

[45] 269 F.3d 305 (4th Cir. 2001), cert. denied, 535 U.S. 986 (2002).

[46] After nearly three decades of court-enforced desegregation, a white parent sued the school district, charging that his daughter had twice been denied admittance to a magnet school

because she was not black. Six other white parents joined the case, arguing that the school district had been successfully rid of segregation and with it any constitutional justification for race-based preferences. The judge agreed, calling the argument for continuing the desegregation process a "bizarre posture" and the focus on racial diversity a "social experiment." The policy of allocating available magnet school spaces to reflect the racial student makeup of the district as a whole was condemned by the court as "nothing more than a means for racial balancing," which could not be justified by a "litany of generalizations lauding the benefits of racial diversity."

47 403 F.3d 246 (5th Cir. 2005).

48 Id. at 259.

49 190 F.3d 1061 (9th Cir. 1999), cert. denied, 531 U.S. 877 (2000).

50 Id. at 1064.

51 Id. at 1065.

52 The holdings in these cases have presumably been invalidated by the Court's subsequent ruling in *Parents Involved in Community Schools*.

53 418 F.3d 1 (1st Cir. 2005).

54 330 F. Supp. 2d 834 (W.D.Ky. 2004).

55 McFarland v. Jefferson County Public Schools, 416 F.3d 513 (6th Cir. 2003).

56 426 F. 3d 1162 (9th Cir. 2005).

57 Comfort v. Lynn Sch. Comm., 418 F.3d 1 (1st Cir. 2005); McFarland v. Jefferson County Pub. Schs., 416 F.3d 513 (6th Cir. 2005); Parents Involved in Cmty. Sch. v. Seattle Sch. Dist., No. 1, 426 F.3d 1162 (9th Cir. 2005).

58 See, e.g., Tuttle v. Arlington County Sch. Bd., 195 F.3d 698 (4th Cir. 1999); Eisenberg ex rel. Eisenberg v. Montgomery County Pub. Schs., 197 F.3d 123 (4th Cir. 1999); Wessmann v. Gittens, 160 F.3d 790 (1st Cir. 1998).

59 547 U.S. 1177 (2006).

60 127 S. Ct. 2738 (2007).

61 Parents Involved in Cmty. Sch. v. Seattle Sch. Dist. No. 1, 127 S. Ct. 2738, 2750-51 (2007).

62 Id. at 2752.

63 Id. at 2754.

64 Id. at 2760.

65 Id. at 2755.

66 Id. at 2757.

67 Id. at 2761-63.

68 347 U.S. 483 (1954).

69 Parents Involved in Cmty. Schs. v. Seattle Sch. Dist. No. 1, 127 S. Ct. at 2768.

70 Id. at 2789.

71 Id. at 2791-92.

72 Id. at 2793.

73 Id. at 2769-70.

74 Id. at 2787.

75 Id. at 2797-800.

76 Id. at 2800.

77 91 F.3d 1547 (3d Cir. 1996), appeal dismissed sub nom. Piscataway Twp. Bd. of Educ. v. Taxman, 522 U.S. 1010 (1997).

78 930 P.2d 730 (Nev. 1997), cert. denied 523 U.S. 1004 (1998).

79 Emily Bazelon, *The Next Kind of Integration*, N.Y. Times, July 20, 2008, at MM38.

80 426 U.S. 229 (1976).

[81] Cf. Personnel Administrator v. Feeney, 442 U.S. 256 (1979). In Feeney, the Court upheld a state law giving a preference to veterans for civil service employment, which had a significant discriminatory effect against female applicants. Notwithstanding the obvious impact of such a preference, the Court upheld it on the ground that "'[d]iscriminatory purpose' ... implies more than intent as volition or intent as awareness of consequences. It implies that the decisionmaker ... selected or reaffirmed a particular course of action at least in part 'because of,' not merely 'in spite of,' its adverse effects upon an identifiable group." Id. at 279. Although Feeney involved a claim of sex-based discrimination, the test there announced for determining whether a purpose is "discriminatory" with respect to a particular trait has been applied to claims of racial discrimination as well. See Hernandez v. New York, 500 U.S. 352, 360 (1991).

[82] United Steelworkers of America v. Weber, 443 U.S. 179 (1979). In Johnson v. Transportation Agency, 480 U.S. 616 (1980), the Court extended this analysis to gender-conscious affirmative action programs in regard to use of a "plus" factor in hiring and promotion decisions.

[83] Wygant v. Board of Education, 476 U.S. 267 (1986).

[84] Patrolmen's Benevolent Assoc. v. City of New York, 310 F.3d 43, 52 (quoting Barhold v. Rodriguez, 863 F.2d 233, 238 (2d Cir. 1988); Reynolds v. City of Chicago, 296 F.3d 524 (7th Cir. 2002). See also Cotter v. City of Boston, 323 F.3d 160, 172 n. 10 (1st Cir. 2003) (declining to address question of compelling interest but expressing sympathy for "the argument that communities place more trust in a diverse police force and that the resulting trust reduces crime rates and improves policing").

In: Affirmative Action and Preferential Treatment ISBN: 978-1-62257-465-0
Editors: P. L. Medina and J. E. Patel 

*Chapter 5*

# RACE DISCRIMINATION AND THE SUPREME COURT: A LEGAL ANALYSIS OF *RICCI V. DESTEFANO*[*]

*Jody Feder*

## SUMMARY

This report discusses *Ricci v. DeStefano*, a recent Supreme Court case involving allegations of reverse discrimination by a group of white firefighters who challenged city officials in New Haven, Connecticut, over their refusal to certify a promotional test on which black and Hispanic firefighters had performed poorly relative to white firefighters. In a 5-4 vote, the Court held that the city's actions violated Title VII of the Civil Rights Act of 1964, which prohibits discrimination in employment on the basis of race, color, religion, sex, or national origin. The case has drawn considerable attention, not only because of the controversial nature of the reverse discrimination allegations but also because the Court reversed a decision by a three-judge appellate panel that included Judge Sonia Sotomayor, who was, at the time, a nominee for the Supreme Court and who has since become a member of the Court.

In June 2009, the Supreme Court issued a decision in *Ricci v. DeStefano*,[1] a case involving allegations of reverse discrimination by a group of white

---

[*] This is an edited, reformatted and augmented version of Congressional Research Service, Publication No. R40697., dated January 19, 2010.

firefighters who challenged city officials in New Haven, Connecticut, over their refusal to certify a promotional test on which black and Hispanic firefighters had performed poorly relative to white firefighters. In a 5-4 vote, the Court held that the city's actions violated Title VII of the Civil Rights Act of 1964, which prohibits discrimination in employment on the basis of race, color, religion, sex, or national origin.[2] The case has drawn considerable attention, not only because of the controversial nature of the reverse discrimination allegations but also because the Court reversed a decision by a three-judge appellate panel that included Judge Sonia Sotomayor,[3] who was, at the time, a nominee for the Supreme Court and who has since become a member of the Court.

## BACKGROUND

In 2003, the City of New Haven administered an examination to determine which firefighters would qualify for promotion to lieutenant and captain positions over the following two years and the order in which they would be considered for promotion. Of the 77 candidates who took the lieutenant examination, 43 were white, 19 were black, and 15 were Hispanic; 25 whites, 6 blacks, and 3 Hispanics passed the exam. Based on the number of lieutenant positions available, the top 10 candidates, all of whom were white, were eligible for promotion. Of the 41 candidates who took the captain examination, 25 were white, 8 were black, and 8 were Hispanic; 16 whites, 3 blacks, and 3 Hispanics passed the test. Based on the number of captain positions available, the top 9 candidates, 7 of whom were white and 2 of whom were Hispanic, were eligible for promotion.[4]

Confronted with the significant racial disparity revealed by the test results, city officials held a series of public meetings to determine whether to certify the exam. Some firefighters, claiming that the statistical disparity demonstrated that the test was racially discriminatory, threatened to sue if the city made promotions based on the test results. Other firefighters argued that the test was fair and threatened to sue if the city denied promotions to the candidates who had performed well. Ultimately, the city declined to certify the exam, and a group primarily composed of white firefighters sued, claiming that the city's actions violated Title VII of the Civil Rights Act and the Equal Protection Clause of the Fourteenth Amendment.

The district court sided with the City of New Haven, holding that the "[d]efendants' motivation to avoid making promotions based on a test with a racially disparate impact ... does not ... as a matter of law, constitute discriminatory intent, and therefore such evidence is insufficient for plaintiffs to prevail on their Title VII claim."[5] Likewise, the district court rejected the plaintiffs' equal protection claim, ruling that the city's attempt to remedy the disparate impact of the test did not constitute an intent to discriminate against the non-minority firefighters and that the rejection of the test results did not amount to an unlawful racial classification because all applicants were treated the same with respect to the administration and invalidation of the tests.[6]

Subsequently, a three-judge panel of the Court of Appeals for the Second Circuit that included Judge Sonia Sotomayor issued a one-paragraph affirmation of the "well-reasoned opinion" of the district court, noting that because the city, "in refusing to validate the exams, was simply trying to fulfill its obligations under Title VII when confronted with test results that had a disproportionate racial impact, its actions were protected."[7] Neither Judge Sotomayor nor the other judges provided additional insight into their legal reasoning in the decision. The Supreme Court granted review in order to consider the Title VII and equal protection claims at issue in the case.

## TITLE VII AND THE EQUAL PROTECTION CLAUSE

Under Title VII, two different types of discrimination are prohibited. The first is disparate treatment,[8] which involves intentional discrimination, such as treating an individual differently because of his or her race. The second type of prohibited discrimination is disparate impact,[9] which involves a neutral employment practice that is not intended to discriminate but that nonetheless has a disproportionate effect on protected individuals. An employer may defend against a disparate impact claim by showing that the challenged practice is "job related for the position in question and consistent with business necessity," although a plaintiff may still succeed by demonstrating that the employer refused to adopt an available alternative employment practice that has less disparate impact and serves the employer's legitimate needs.[10]

Under the Equal Protection Clause of the Fourteenth Amendment, "[n]o state shall ... deny to any person within its jurisdiction the equal protection of the laws."[11] To maintain an equal protection challenge, government action must be established; that is, it must be shown that the government, and not a private actor, has acted in a discriminatory manner. Although the Fourteenth

Amendment requires equal protection, it does not preclude the classification of individuals. A classification will not offend the Constitution unless it is characterized by invidious discrimination.[12] Over the years, the Court has interpreted the equal protection clause in a way that requires different degrees of scrutiny for such classifications, depending on the category of persons affected. Under the strict scrutiny test, which is the most stringent form of review and applies to classifications based on race, the government must show that the classification drawn by a statute is narrowly tailored to meet a compelling governmental interest.[13]

The question that arose in *Ricci* was whether the city's failure to certify the test results violated Title VII's prohibition against disparate treatment or the constitutional requirement for equal protection. The firefighters who sued argued that the city's refusal to promote them constituted discrimination on the basis of race in violation of both Title VII and the Equal Protection Clause. City officials defended their actions, arguing that the city was attempting to comply with Title VII and avoid a lawsuit when it refused to certify test results that had a disparate impact on minority firefighters. The Supreme Court granted review to resolve the dispute.

## THE SUPREME COURT'S DECISION

Ultimately, the Court ruled in favor of the white firefighters, holding that the city had violated Title VII's prohibition against disparate treatment when it discarded the test results. According to Justice Kennedy, who wrote the majority opinion,[14] the city's rejection of the racially disparate exam results was, despite its seemingly well-intentioned attempt to avoid disparate impact liability, an explicitly race-based decision that would violate the disparate treatment prohibition in the absence of a valid defense. In order to reconcile what the majority viewed as two competing provisions of Title VII, the Court established a new standard — imported from its equal protection jurisprudence — for evaluating when attempts to avoid disparate impact liability excuse what otherwise would be prohibited disparate treatment under Title VII. According to the Court, "before an employer can engage in intentional discrimination for the asserted purpose of avoiding or remedying an unintentional disparate impact, the employer must have a strong basis in evidence to believe it will be subject to disparate-impact liability if it fails to take the race-conscious, discriminatory action."[15] The Court explained:

> Applying the strong-basis-in-evidence standard to Title VII gives effect to both the disparate-treatment and disparate-impact provisions, allowing violations of one in the name of compliance with the other only in certain, narrow circumstances. The standard leaves ample room for employers' voluntary compliance efforts, which are essential to the statutory scheme and to Congress's efforts to eradicate workplace discrimination. And the standard appropriately constrains employers' discretion in making race-based decisions: It limits that discretion to cases in which there is a strong basis in evidence of disparate-impact liability, but it is not so restrictive that it allows employers to act only when there is a provable, actual violation.[16]

Applying this new standard, the Court found that the city did not have a strong basis in evidence to conclude that the promotion examination would constitute a disparate impact violation. Although the minority firefighters could have established a prima facie case of disparate impact based on the statistical results of the test, such a showing is not sufficient to establish a violation of Title VII. Rather, the city would have been liable only if the tests were not job-related and consistent with business necessity or if a less discriminatory alternative that would have met the fire department's needs was not adopted. The Court held that there was no evidence that the tests were not job-related or that there was a less discriminatory test available and therefore the city lacked a strong basis in evidence for believing that it would be subject to disparate impact liability.[17] Because the case was ultimately decided on statutory grounds, the Court did not reach the constitutional question related to the firefighters' Equal Protection claim.

Two justices filed concurring opinions in the case. Justice Scalia, writing for himself, indicated that Title VII's disparate impact provisions may warrant closer constitutional scrutiny. Although Justice Scalia agreed that it was unnecessary to reach the constitutional question in the current case, he noted that the Court's "resolution of this dispute merely postpones the evil day on which the Court will have to confront the question: Whether, or to what extent, are the disparate-impact provisions of Title VII of the Civil Rights Act of 1964 consistent with the Constitution's guarantee of equal protection?"[18] Justice Alito also wrote a concurring opinion in which he was joined by Justices Scalia and Thomas. The primary purpose of Justice Alito's opinion appeared to be to rebut several arguments made by the dissenting Justices, particularly the dissent's interpretation of the evidentiary record.[19]

Justice Ginsburg, writing for the dissent, criticized the Court's opinion, arguing that it failed to recognize the "centrality of the disparate-impact concept to effective enforcement of Title VII" and the legacy of race discrimination in the firefighting profession.[20] In addition, the dissenting justices, disagreeing with the notion that Title VII's disparate impact and disparate treatment provisions stand in conflict, rejected the Court's newly established "strong basis in evidence" standard. Rather, the dissenting justices would have held that an employer who discards a policy or practice that has a disparate impact does not violate Title VII's prohibition against disparate treatment, as long as the employer has good cause to believe the policy or practice is not a business necessity.[21] Because "New Haven had ample cause to believe its selection process was flawed and not justified by business necessity," the dissenting justices would have held that the city did not violate Title VII.[22]

In the wake of the Court's ruling, the U.S. District Court for the District of Connecticut, to which the case had been remanded for entry of judgment, issued an order instructing state officials to promote the firefighters who had sued.[23]

## Significance of the Decision

The Court's decision in *Ricci* is likely to affect the workplace in several different ways. Although employees will still be able to bring Title VII disparate impact claims against their employers, the decision will make it more difficult for employers to voluntarily comply with Title VII by altering employment policies or practices that have an unintentionally discriminatory effect. Perhaps more importantly, the decision also signals that laws that prohibit disparate impact discrimination may face increasing constitutional scrutiny in the future, a trend that could fundamentally alter the current structure of Title VII and several other civil rights laws, as well as significantly limit the ability of employees to sue for unintentional discrimination.

In addition, the *Ricci* decision has implications for Congress. Since *Ricci* was decided on statutory grounds, legislators who disagree with the Court's interpretation could introduce legislation that overturns the new "strong basis in evidence" standard or that provides an exception to the statutory prohibition against disparate treatment in the case of disparate impact. Such congressional action is not uncommon, particularly in the civil rights context. For example, the 111$^{th}$ Congress recently passed the Lilly Ledbetter Fair Pay Act of 2009,[24] which superseded the Court's 2007 decision in *Ledbetter v. Goodyear Tire & Rubber Co., Inc.*[25] The difficulty for Congress, however, is that such legislation could potentially be subject to constitutional challenge if it offends the Equal Protection Clause's prohibition against disparate treatment and fails to pass the strict scrutiny test.

Finally, as noted above, the Court's ruling in *Ricci* overturned a Second Circuit decision in which Judge Sotomayor participated. Although the Court's ruling did not appear to significantly affect her nomination, it is important to note that this new standard was not in effect when the Second Circuit issued its decision in the *Ricci* case and therefore could not have been applied by Judge Sotomayor or her colleagues at the time that they ruled in the case.

## End Notes

[1] 129 S. Ct. 2658 (2009).
[2] 42 U.S.C. § 2000e-2(a).
[3] For more information on Judge Sotomayor's decision in *Ricci* and other civil rights cases, see CRS Report R40649, *Judge Sonia Sotomayor: Analysis of Selected Opinions*, coordinated by Anna C. Henning and Kenneth R. Thomas.
[4] Ricci v. DeStefano, 129 S. Ct. 2658, 2666 (2009).
[5] Ricci v. DeStefano, 554 F. Supp. 2d 142, 160 (D. Conn. 2006).
[6] *Id.* at 161-62.
[7] Ricci v. DeStefano, 530 F.3d at 87 (2d Cir. 2008).
[8] 42 U.S.C. § 2000e-2(a)(1).
[9] Id. at § 2000e-2(k).
[10] Id.
[11] U.S. Const. amend. XIV, § 1.
[12] *See* Ferguson v. Skrupa, 372 U.S. 726, 732 (1963).
[13] *See* San Antonio Independent School District v. Rodriquez, 411 U.S. 1 (1973).
[14] Justices Roberts, Scalia, Thomas, and Alito joined in the majority opinion.
[15] Ricci v. DeStefano, 129 S. Ct. 2658, 2677 (2009).
[16] Id. at 2676.
[17] Id. at 2677-78.
[18] Id. at 2681-82.
[19] Id. at 2683-89.
[20] Id. at 2690. Justice Ginsburg was joined in dissent by Justices Stevens, Souter, and Breyer.
[21] Id. at 2699.
[22] Id. at 2703.
[23] Ricci v. DeStefano, No. 3:04cv1109 (D. Conn. November 24, 2009), available at http://www.ctemploymentlawblog.com/uploads/file/ricciorder1124.pdf.
[24] P.L. 111-2.
[25] 550 U.S. 618 (2007).

In: Affirmative Action and Preferential Treatment ISBN: 978-1-62257-465-0
Editors: P. L. Medina and J. E. Patel 

*Chapter 6*

# PAY DISCRIMINATION CLAIMS UNDER TITLE VII OF THE CIVIL RIGHTS ACT: A LEGAL ANALYSIS OF THE SUPREME COURT'S DECISION IN *LEDBETTER V. GOODYEAR TIRE & RUBBER CO., INC.*[*]

*Jody Feder*

## SUMMARY

This report discusses *Ledbetter v. Goodyear Tire & Rubber Co., Inc.*, a case in which the Supreme Court considered the timeliness of a sex discrimination claim filed under Title VII of the Civil Rights Act, which prohibits employment discrimination on the basis of race, color, religion, sex, or national origin. In *Ledbetter*, the female plaintiff alleged that past sex discrimination had resulted in lower pay increases and that these past pay decisions continued to affect the amount of her pay throughout her employment, resulting in a significant pay disparity between her and her male colleagues by the end of her nearly 20-year career. Under Title VII, a plaintiff is required to file suit within 180 days after an alleged unlawful employment practice has occurred. Although the plaintiff in *Ledbetter* argued that each paycheck she received constituted a new violation of the statute and therefore reset the clock with regard to filing a claim, the

* This is an edited, reformatted and augmented version of Congressional Research Service, Publication No. RS22686, dated April 29, 2009.

Court rejected this argument, reasoning that even if employees suffer continuing effects from past discrimination, their claims are time barred unless filed within the specified number of days of the original discriminatory act. On January 29, 2009, President Obama signed the Lilly Ledbetter Fair Pay Act of 2009 (H.R. 11/S. 181). This legislation supersedes the *Ledbetter* decision by amending Title VII to clarify that the time limit for suing employers for pay discrimination begins each time they issue a paycheck.

In June 2007, the Supreme Court issued its decision in *Ledbetter v. Goodyear Tire & Rubber Co., Inc.*,[1] a case that involved questions about the timeliness of claims filed under Title VII of the Civil Rights Act, which prohibits discrimination in employment on the basis of race, color, religion, sex, or national origin.[2] By a 5-4 vote margin, the Court rejected the plaintiff's argument that each paycheck she received reflected a lower salary due to past discrimination and therefore constituted a new violation of the statute. Instead, the Court held that "a new violation does not occur, and a new charging period does not commence, upon the occurrence of subsequent nondiscriminatory acts that entail adverse effects resulting from the past discrimination."[3] As a result, the Court held that the plaintiff had not filed suit in a timely manner. Initially, the decision appeared to limit some pay discrimination claims based on Title VII, but did not affect an individual's ability to sue for sex discrimination that results in pay bias under the Equal Pay Act. Although the Court's decision made it more difficult for employees to sue for pay discrimination under Title VII, the decision was recently superseded by the Lilly Ledbetter Fair Pay Act of 2009, which amended Title VII to clarify that the time limit for suing employers for pay discrimination begins each time they issue a paycheck.[4]

## BACKGROUND

From 1979 until 1998, Lilly Ledbetter worked as a supervisor for the Goodyear Tire & Rubber Company. Although Ledbetter initially received a salary similar to the salaries paid to her male colleagues, a pay disparity developed over time. By 1997, the pay disparity between Ledbetter and her 15 male counterparts had widened considerably, to the point that Ledbetter was paid $3,727 per month while the lowest paid male colleague received $4,286 per month and the highest-paid male colleague received $5,236 per month.

In 1998, Ledbetter filed a charge of discrimination with the Equal Employment Opportunity Commission (EEOC) alleging that Goodyear had unlawfully discriminated against her on the basis of her sex in violation of Title VII. According to Ledbetter, her current pay was discriminatorily low due to a long series of decisions reflecting Goodyear's pervasive discrimination against female managers in general and Ledbetter in particular. A jury found in her favor, and the district court entered judgment for backpay and damages,[5] but the appellate court reversed.[6] The Supreme Court granted review in order to resolve disagreement among the appellate courts regarding the proper application of the time limit for filing claims in Title VII disparate treatment pay cases.[7]

## TITLE VII AND FILING DEADLINES FOR DISCRIMINATION CLAIMS

Under Title VII, it is an "unlawful employment practice" for an employer to discriminate "against any individual with respect to his compensation ... because of such individual's race, color, religion, sex, or national origin."[8] Individuals who want to challenge an employment practice as unlawful are required to file a charge with the EEOC within a specified period—either 180 days or 300 days, depending on the state—"after the alleged unlawful employment practice occurred."[9]

The question that arose in the *Ledbetter* case was how to determine precisely what types of activities constitute an unlawful employment practice for purposes of starting the clock on the filing deadline. Ledbetter argued that two different employment practices could qualify as having occurred within the 180-day charging period preceding the filing of her EEOC claim: (1) the paychecks that were issued to her during that period, each of which she alleged constituted a separate act of discrimination, or (2) a 1998 decision denying her a raise, which she contended was unlawful because it perpetuated the discriminatory pay decisions from previous years. In contrast, Goodyear argued that Ledbetter's claim was time barred because the discriminatory acts that affected her current pay had taken place prior to the 180 days that preceded the claim Ledbetter filed with the EEOC. The Supreme Court granted review to resolve the dispute.

# THE SUPREME COURT'S DECISION

Ultimately, the Supreme Court ruled in favor of Goodyear, holding that Ledbetter's suit was time barred because no unlawfully discriminatory acts had taken place within the 180-day charging period. In rejecting Ledbetter's claim on statutory grounds, the Court majority relied heavily on the principle that Title VII claims alleging disparate treatment require evidence of discriminatory intent. Because there was no evidence that Goodyear had acted with discriminatory intent when it issued the paychecks Ledbetter received during the charging period or when the company had denied her a raise in 1998, the Court found that Goodyear had not engaged in an unlawful employment practice during the specified time period. As a result, the fact that Ledbetter may have been suffering from the continuing effects of past discrimination was not sufficient for her to establish a claim within the statutorily mandated filing period.[10]

In issuing its decision, the *Ledbetter* majority relied on a series of precedents in analogous employment discrimination cases. For example, one such case, *United Air Lines, Inc. v. Evans*,[11] involved a female flight attendant who was not granted seniority when she was rehired despite the fact that she had originally been forced to resign when she got married. Although the Court agreed that the company's discriminatory policy had a continuing effect, that effect was not sufficient to establish a present violation. Similarly, in *Lorance v. AT&T Technologies, Inc.*,[12] the Court rejected a challenge to a discriminatory seniority system because the complaint had been filed when the discriminatory effect was felt, rather than within the charging period established by the original discriminatory act, namely the adoption of the seniority system. In light of these and other precedents, the Court concluded:

> The EEOC charging period is triggered when a discrete unlawful practice takes place. A new violation does not occur, and a new charging period does not commence, upon the occurrence of subsequent nondiscriminatory acts that entail adverse effects resulting from the past discrimination. But of course, if an employer engages in a series of acts each of which is intentionally discriminatory, then a fresh violation takes place when each act is committed.... [C]urrent effects alone cannot breathe life into prior, uncharged discrimination....[13]

Of primary concern to the Court was the question of discriminatory intent. In general, claims such as Ledbetter's, which allege unlawful disparate treatment, must demonstrate discriminatory intent. According to the Court, allowing Ledbetter to shift the intent associated with the discriminatory pay decisions to later paychecks would have the effect of imposing liability in the absence of the required intent.[14] The Court also appeared concerned that allowing Ledbetter's claim to proceed would undermine Title VII enforcement procedures and filing deadlines, which were designed in part to protect employers from defending against discrimination claims that are long past. According to the Court, Title VII's short filing deadline "reflects Congress' strong preference for the prompt resolution of employment discrimination allegations through voluntary conciliation and cooperation."[15]

The Court also rejected Ledbetter's reliance on *Bazemore v. Friday*,[16] a pay discrimination case involving employees who were, prior to enactment of Title VII, separated into a white branch and a black branch, with the latter group receiving lower salaries. Although the *Bazemore* Court held that an employer who adopts a discriminatory pay structure violates Title VII whenever it issues a paycheck to disfavored employees, the *Ledbetter* Court distinguished the two cases, arguing that the paychecks in *Bazemore* reflected the employer's ongoing retention of a discriminatory pay structure—a current violation of the statute—while the paychecks in Ledbetter reflected the continuing effect of an isolated, past violation of the statute.[17] Finally, although the EEOC has interpreted Title VII to allow challenges based on discriminatory pay each time a paycheck is received,[18] the Court declined to defer to the agency's interpretation.[19]

In contrast, the dissent in *Ledbetter* strongly disagreed with the majority's analysis. According to the dissent, treating the actual payment of a discriminatory wage as an unlawful employment practice would be more faithful to precedent, would better reflect workplace realities, and would be more consistent with the overall purpose of Title VII. Specifically, the dissent argued that the Court's holding was inconsistent with the result in *Bazemore*, contending that *Bazemore* recognized that paychecks that perpetuate past discrimination constitute a fresh instance of discrimination every time they are issued.[20] The dissent also drew an analogy between pay discrimination claims and sexual harassment hostile work environment claims, which involve a series of discrete acts that recur and are cumulative in impact. Since hostile work environment claims may be filed even when some of the discrete acts that form the basis for a claim have taken place outside of the charging period, the dissent would have allowed Ledbetter's claim to proceed as well.[21]

The dissent also distinguished pay bias claims from other types of employment discrimination, arguing that pay discrimination is fundamentally different from other types of employment bias. For example, employees, who are generally aware when they suffer adverse employment actions related to promotion, transfer, hiring, or firing, may not know they have suffered pay discrimination, particularly because salary levels are often hidden from the employee's view and pay disparities become apparent only over time. As a result of these differences, the dissent argued that the precedents upon which the Court relied were inapplicable because those cases involved easily identifiable acts of discrimination.[22] Finally, the dissent criticized the majority's opinion as inconsistent with the overall anti-discrimination purpose of Title VII.

## EFFECT OF THE DECISION

Although the *Ledbetter* decision was subsequently overturned by statute, at the time of the ruling, many commentators noted the possible effects that the case could have on the workplace. First, employees might have had a more difficult time bringing pay discrimination claims under Title VII. If employees brought pay discrimination claims early in order to meet the statutory filing deadline, they might have had difficulty proving discrimination if the pay disparity remained small. If employees brought pay discrimination claims later, however, then they might not have been able to meet the filing deadline. As a result of this dilemma, employers might have experienced an increase in pay discrimination claims being filed against them, since some employees might have filed claims in order to meet the deadline even in cases where discrimination was unclear.

It is also important to note that the *Ledbetter* decision affected more than just pay bias cases involving sex discrimination. Because Title VII applies to discrimination on the basis of race, color, national origin, sex, and religion, many other classes of claimants were potentially affected by the decision. Furthermore, the *Ledbetter* case also affected pay discrimination under parallel employment discrimination statutes that are patterned on Title VII, such as the Age Discrimination in Employment Act (ADEA), the Rehabilitation Act of 1973, and the Americans with Disabilities Act (ADA). Employees who filed pay discrimination claims alleging race or age discrimination, for example, might have been more negatively affected by the decision than employees who alleged sex discrimination because the latter group still had recourse under the Equal Pay Act (EPA).

The EPA, which prohibits discrimination on the basis of sex with regard to the compensation paid to men and women for substantially equal work performed in the same establishment,[23] does contain a statute of limitations for filing claims but has, thus far, been interpreted in such a way that each issuance of an unequal paycheck is treated as a new discriminatory act.[24]

In addition, the *Ledbetter* decision spurred congressional efforts to overturn the ruling. Since *Ledbetter* was decided on statutory grounds, several legislators who disagreed with the Court's interpretation introduced legislation clarifying that unlawful employment practices under Title VII include each issuance of a paycheck that reflects a discriminatory compensation practice. Such congressional action is not uncommon. For example, the *Lorance* decision, cited as precedent by the *Ledbetter* majority, was subsequently superseded by Congress in the Civil Rights Act of 1991.[25]

After the *Ledbetter* decision was handed down, several bills to amend Title VII in light of the opinion were introduced in both the 110th and 111th congressional sessions. As passed by Congress and signed into law by President Obama on January 29, 2009,[26] the Lilly Ledbetter Fair Pay Act of 2009 (H.R. 11/S. 181) clarifies that the time limit for suing employers for pay discrimination begins each time they issue a paycheck and is not limited to the original discriminatory action.[27] This change is applicable not only to Title VII of the Civil Rights Act, but also to the Age Discrimination in Employment Act (ADEA), the Rehabilitation Act of 1973, and the Americans with Disabilities Act (ADA).

## End Notes

[1] 550 U.S. 618 (2007).
[2] 42 U.S.C. § 2000e-2(a).
[3] Ledbetter v. Goodyear Tire & Rubber Co., 550 U.S. 618, 628 (2007).
[4] P.L. 111-2.
[5] 2003 U.S. Dist. LEXIS 27406 (D. Ala. 2003).
[6] 421 F.3d 1169 (11th Cir. 2005).
[7] 548 U.S. 903 (2006).
[8] 42 U.S.C. § 2000e-2(a).
[9] Id. at § 2000e-2(a)(1).
[10] 550 U.S. 618, 625 (2007).
[11] 431 U.S. 553 (1977).
[12] 490 U.S. 900 (1989).
[13] Ledbetter, 550 U.S. at 628.
[14] Id. at 629.
[15] Id. at 630-31.

[16] 478 U.S. 385 (1986).

[17] Ledbetter, 550 U.S. at 633-37.

[18] EEOC Compliance Manual §2-IV-C(1)(a), http://www.eeoc.gov/policy/docs/threshold.html.

[19] Ledbetter, 550 U.S. at 643, n. 11.

[20] Id. at 646-47.

[21] Id. at 647-49.

[22] Id. at 649-52.

[23] 29 U.S.C. § 206. For more information on pay discrimination laws, including the EPA, see CRS Report RL31867, *Pay Equity Legislation*, by Jody Feder and Linda Levine.

[24] See, e.g., Cardenas v. Massey, 269 F.3d 251 (3d Cir. 2001).

[25] P.L. 102-166.

[26] P.L. 111-2.

[27] It is important to note that the House-passed version of H.R. 11 incorporated the text of the Paycheck Fairness Act (H.R. 12), a separate bill that would amend the Equal Pay Act, but the Senate bill did not. As a result, the House took up S. 181 for a final vote.

# INDEX

## B



## C

## D



## E

## F

## O



## P

## Q



## R



## S

**V**



**W**



**Y**